ABCs OF RELATIONSHIPS

Originally Copyrighted © 2006 by

Cynthia Moore
Inner Harmony Books
PO Box 16783
Sugar Land, TX 77496

I0170806

Editing, Cover and Layout Designed by Kitty Y. Williams

Front and Back Cover Images Courtesy of
© Can Stock Photo Inc: /4774344sean and /Arcady

2nd Edition/Printing. Copyright © 2014 Inner Harmony Books
ISBN 978-0-9789961-2-3 Paperback

Printed in the United States of America.

About the Author

Cynthia Moore has a Master's of Science in Counseling Psychology and is a Licensed Professional Counselor in the state of Texas. She has worked with various populations in the mental health field that include:

- Clinical Director and Coordinator - Residential Treatment Centers for Children, Adolescents, and Young Adults.

- Partial Hospitalization - Dual Diagnosed Adults with both severe Mental Illness and Chemical Dependency.

- Inpatient Hospitalization - Adults, Children and Adolescents.

- Intensive Outpatient Program - Mental Health Adult Intensive Groups.

- Lead Clinician - Assertive Community Treatment - Psychosocial Rehabilitation Mental Health Outpatient Adult Population.

- Practice Manager of two Mental Health Outpatient Clinics.

- Care Advocate Behavioral Utilization Management.

- Private Practice.

Acknowledgments

Thanks to my children, relatives, friends and colleagues, who donated their time to listen, read and provide comments for the *ABCs of Relationships: Emotional Survival Games* book. I am also very grateful to my children who gave their honest feedback on my interaction as a parent with them that ultimately contributed to their adult lives.

I especially would like to thank two of my long term friends and colleagues, Nurse Helena Thomas and Licensed Marriage & Family Therapist (LMFT) Darlene Gibbs, for their objective feedback, encouragement and support throughout the first edition of this book. Their combined feedback provided me the courage needed to develop and complete the second edition.

Finally, thanks to my mother and father, who always promoted by worth and cheered my endeavors.

Table of Contents

Introduction

Surviving the adult world is very challenging. Without a healthy emotional foundation, our interactions with each other are very child-like in nature and we fail to communicate our true needs, desires, or to obtain and sustain our goals. We ultimately crash into each other the same as two cars driving on the wrong side of the road. Then we are left pondering on what went wrong, or if we are not good enough. The goal of *ABCs of Relationships: Emotional Survival Games* is to provide helpful insight and details about barriers and dilemmas that prevent us from maximizing our true potential in this life or aligning and bonding with compatible partners.

Joan and Jim

As Jim and Joan finished making love, Joan abruptly got up and ran to the bathroom. Jim shouted out, *"What is wrong with you? You are acting as if you did not like it. Girl, you need to loosen up!"* Joan slowly sat on the floor and blurted out, *"You wore me out!"* Jim roared with laughter as he shouted back, *"It has been a while since we have been together."*

Joan regretted hanging out with Jim again and sat quietly on the floor questioning why she continued to do this to herself; however, she was relieved to hear that Jim had not been with anyone else since their last encounter because they did not use protection. She then heard him snoring very loudly and decided to stay in the bathroom a bit longer. Joan reflected on conversations she has had with her best friend and co-worker Nina, regarding what she saw in Jim and how long she planned on putting up with this arrangement. After all, it had been five years of *"He loves me, he loves me not..."*

Joan could hear herself over and over justifying her interactions with Jim by telling Nina that being with him was better than not having anyone at all, regardless of his coldness, aloofness and his lack of attentiveness. She had also told Nina that Jim was a good man and possibly loved her, but was confused.

She continued to reflect on Nina's response and could hear her screaming with loud laughter of disbelief, *"Confused? Girl please, this is not the first time that you have been in this situation. Remember Broderick? Then there were the Wilson and Murphy episodes, and now Jim."* She could also hear Nina go on and on about her being a very attractive, professional woman with a career, house and taking care of herself just fine.

Nina would scream, *"Girl, what is going on with you? You act as if you are getting what you want from this man! I thought you wanted someone who loved, genuinely cared and was willing to spend quality time with you. Maybe you need to see one of those talk doctors because this is not the confident woman that I know."* Although Joan knew Nina was right, she hated those logical conversations but still lacked the emotional willpower to resist hanging out with Jim. As Joan further reflected on many ways that she had compromised her values to keep Jim in her life, she vaguely agreed that Nina may be right and that something was wrong with her.

As Joan questioned if her rationality was somehow lost in her emotions, she heard Jim call her name explaining that he needed to leave. Hastily getting up from the floor she softly asked him why he needed to leave so soon given that it was the weekend. Jim responded with his usual comment, *"Too busy to stay."* Joan then asked him about going to dinner or a movie sometime. Jim told her *"Maybe."* He then gave her a kiss on the forehead and quickly left.

Joan hated those kisses on her forehead and once told Nina it made her feel like a hopeless child who was begging and hoping her daddy would spend time with her. She slowly walked to the sofa and began weeping, reflecting on why she continues to find herself strongly attracted to individuals for whom she would compromise and go against her standards, morals and best judgment. Joan was baffled at her own judgment as if she had completely forgotten the other compromises.

Joan is not alone in this same old relationship scenario where we fall hard for someone and then compromise our values. Many of us, just like her, also often find ourselves in cycles of strong attractions, compromises, regretful judgments, and ultimately unfulfilling relationships.

Take Daniel for example who was a really sweet and nice guy, but also had a hard time letting go of his girlfriend Sheryl who repeatedly cheated on him. He had been stuck in this cycle for five years before realizing that all of his time investments had not been reciprocated. During their five year relationship she had cheated on him at least seven times.

Each time she was caught by Daniel, Sheryl would plead for his forgiveness and vow that it would never happen again. Daniel of course being a very forgiving guy who truly loved her, would forgive her then shortly afterwards find himself in the same scenario again.

The Attraction between Joan and Jim

Let's do the math and look closely at the attraction between Joan and Jim, and why they both felt strongly compelled to continue seeing each other in spite of two different motives; or were their motives the same? Joan would admit that Jim communicated up front he was not interested in a committed relationship with her. Jim would acknowledge that it appeared Joan was becoming more and more attached as time passed and had made several hints of a long term relationship with him.

So if Jim, who did not want a committed relationship, was aware of Joan's increasing attachment why did he continue to have sex with her? Was he confused as Joan suspected? Or better yet was this the only woman with whom Jim could get his physical needs met? What needs was he getting met by continuing this unbalanced exchange? What about Joan? Was something really wrong with her as Nina suggested as she continued to have sex with Jim in spite of feeling used and confused when the sexual exchange was over? Joan decided it was time to find out if something was wrong with her and took Nina up on her suggestion of consulting with a talk doctor.

I know by now you are probably starting to think about your own attractions to others and maybe are squinting your eyes at compromises you have made. It's ok, we have all done it so you are not alone. Instead of losing those thoughts, I want to give you a chance to capture them. Before we see the outcome of Joan's therapy consultation regarding her dilemma with Jim, pause for a moment and jot down any thoughts that came to your mind thus far. Then take a brief look at how you interact with others in intimate, work and social relationships by completing a quick survey.

CAPTURE YOUR THOUGHTS ABOUT
ATTRACTIONS TO OTHERS

PRE-SURVEY

1. I have adjusted and compromised my values to align, bond and connect to others.

Strongly Agree   Agree   Sometimes   Disagree   Strongly Disagree

2. I have often misinterpreted others' responses into my own fantasized value of their intentions with me.

Strongly Agree   Agree   Sometimes   Disagree   Strongly Disagree

3. I have often had sex to avoid being alone.

Strongly Agree   Agree   Sometimes   Disagree   Strongly Disagree

4. I need to have discussions with others on how to interact with a person.

Strongly Agree   Agree   Sometimes   Disagree   Strongly Disagree

5. I have repeatedly tried to align, bond, connect and commit myself to others without success.

Strongly Agree   Agree   Sometimes   Disagree   Strongly Disagree

6. I have often asked myself what is wrong with me.

Strongly Agree   Agree   Sometimes   Disagree   Strongly Disagree

7. I feel a need to survive or plan a strategy in upcoming interactions with others.

Strongly Agree   Agree   Sometimes   Disagree   Strongly Disagree

8. I participate in gossiping.

Strongly Agree   Agree   Sometimes   Disagree   Strongly Disagree

9. I often say that I am too busy to go out or participate in events.

Strongly Agree   Agree   Sometimes   Disagree   Strongly Disagree

10. I talk excessively on the telephone to avoid being alone.

Strongly Agree   Agree   Sometimes   Disagree   Strongly Disagree

11. I have never cheated on my mate not even once.

Strongly Agree   Agree   Sometimes   Disagree   Strongly Disagree

12. I am aware of my challenges and weakness in relationships.

Strongly Agree   Agree   Sometimes   Disagree   Strongly Disagree

13. I do not lie to others to avoid uncomfortable situations.

Strongly Agree   Agree   Sometimes   Disagree   Strongly Disagree

14. I am aware of my strengths in relationships.

Strongly Agree   Agree   Sometimes   Disagree   Strongly Disagree

15. I am aware of my emotional vulnerabilities in relationships.

Strongly Agree   Agree   Sometimes   Disagree   Strongly Disagree

16. I am aware of the impact of my family of origin experience in my interaction with others.

Strongly Agree   Agree   Sometimes   Disagree   Strongly Disagree

17. I feel secure with my emotions as I interact with others.

Strongly Agree   Agree   Sometimes   Disagree   Strongly Disagree

18. I have remained faithful to my values and standards as I have tried to align, bond and connect with others.

Strongly Agree   Agree   Sometimes   Disagree   Strongly Disagree

19. I do not need others to validate my decisions.

Strongly Agree   Agree   Sometimes   Disagree   Strongly Disagree

20. I have settled in relationships to avoid being alone.

Strongly Agree   Agree   Sometimes   Disagree   Strongly Disagree

Keep this survey in mind as you continue to read. We will revisit this and review the outcome later.

ABCs of Emotional Vulnerability

So Joan goes to therapy and after about eight sessions, learned that she had emotional vulnerabilities that were impairing her ability to use good judgment in her interactions with Jim and others from past relationships. As a result of her vulnerabilities, she unintentionally played emotional survival games in dealing with Jim and others to compensate for losses related to her early childhood experiences. Joan learned that those experiences left her in emotional distress, provoked by her internal low self-worth. Unfortunately she did not receive the appropriate assistance from her parents to deal with those issues.

Her parents had made the same mistakes that lots of parents make. They believed that if their children were meeting physical and intellectual developmental milestones, then they were okay. However as we evolve from one conscious level to the next, we are becoming more and more aware that we are missing something beyond intellectual, and physical development to sustain our relationships, hopes and dreams. Now I grant you all of that is important, but not exclusive of emotional development for a well balanced life. The point here is to promote both parents' abilities and responsibilities to teach and model emotional liability in order to cope with life's challenges in a world of good and evil; it is as crucial as promoting intellectual, athletic and physical development. Joan felt better learning that nothing was wrong with her and she was not alone in her relationship dilemma.

Emotional vulnerability is very pervasive across many cultures and class status to the point where the private issues of Presidents, Preachers, Policemen, Physicians, Senators, as well as those of the nice guy or sweet girl next door have been exposed in the public arena. As Joan sat back and thought more about it, she realized that she lacked the confidence to move on from Jim, which was associated with her internal beliefs about herself and affiliating emotions that contributed to the games.

The more and more Joan understood the relationship between her adult behaviors in reaction to internal thoughts and the related emotional distress, she suddenly had an epiphany that Jim was also stagnated in his own vulnerabilities and was also playing emotional survival games with her. Otherwise, logically at least, he would have either committed or moved on and discontinued to have sex with her, knowing that she really wanted to take the relationship further.

Joan was now ready to interrupt the games by identifying and exploring in detail the characteristics of her thoughts and the games she had played to align, and bond with Jim and others. Put on your goggles and oxygen mask as we first deeply explore the underuurrent attraction between Jim and Joan; and second we'll learn how their emotional vulnerabilities played a significant role in their compelling need to continue seeing each other in spite of not getting what they each wanted from their interactions.

Sexual attraction was the core of their relationship, at least for Jim. Joan reached the conclusion that although she had viewed sex as an expression of closeness and intense passion between the two of them, for her it was a profound act towards a long-term commitment with him. The value she placed on sex is where they clashed and became stagnated as a result of their own personal interpretations. During her sessions, Joan uncovered that the content of their attraction contained positive verbiage and physical feel goods that she had associated to her inner self worth. She also finally recognized that by the time she and Jim had reached early adulthood, they both had been ingrained with so much information from their upbringings, that they now had many programmed beliefs regarding their self-worth, sense of belonging and their abilities.

Joan began realizing that in spite of hers and Jim's abilities to obtain great education and careers, they both had very tough emotional childhood experiences that left them with hurt and damaged emotions; they were unable to healthily bond with others. She remembered the Therapist had explained that the role of the primary caregivers is very crucial in nurturing the emotional lives of young children and adolescents. As she continued to reflect on her upbringing, Joan figured out that although not intentional, her father had either overlooked, minimized or dismissed this responsibility to her mother. Joan was filled with mixed emotions as she reflected on various news reports she'd heard over the years where both parents abandoned this responsibility altogether. They often left their children on their own to handle issues far too big for their little minds and souls to process or even left them in the hands of strangers who may or may not hurt them. Joan realized that out of all the times she had thought about being a mother, she had never thought about the term "*Emotional Development*". Now she was rethinking her whole set of expectations for Jim and pondering over his ability to be the father of her children given his emotional unavailability to her.

As Joan continued to master her understanding of emotional vulnerability, she first concluded that she and Jim had subsequently, both unknowingly played the sexual affection game to comfort themselves and relieve underlying emotional distress. Second, their thoughts and emotions had already formed a relationship early on in life that dictated their interactions. In other words, whatever they thought, they felt and behaved accordingly to their vulnerable emotions. Third, in spite of Jim's behaviors toward her, Joan did not think she was worthy of anything better and therefore played a <u>hoping and wishing game</u> with herself and reacted with behaviors that were not age appropriate. Fourth, her judgment to continue having sex with Jim despite knowing he did not want anything more, was based on her emotional age; it was like that of a young innocent child in a make believe storyline hoping daddy or mommy will come for a visit. Now all of this was a bit much for her to swallow, but she did what needed to be done in order to get through her therapy sessions.

Joan was absolutely right regarding not being alone. Many folks silently struggle with giving their heart and mind to someone who is not committed to them in a <u>together forever relationship.</u> Just think about that for a second and you may even hear the echoes of yourself saying the same as Nina, "*Why do you keep seeing him/her? I do not understand.*" The truth is we meet people who we think are ideal for us and if they melt a real good kiss on us, our logic buckles and limps right out the door. We lose sight of what is in our best interest because it felt so good and accepting of us. So now we think this is the one to <u>rescue us from the relationship salvage yard.</u> I know "salvage yard" is a little brutal for some, but it is the reality of how some of us manage our self-worth when trying to align with others. It is as if we have been put out into a pasture waiting and hoping for a rider to help us feel connected to society. Then with the first person that comes by and acts interested, we bow down and let them ride anyway they want, just to have a rider; instead of kicking and bucking them away and saying "*Wrong ride buddy.*"

Hopefully you can clearly see by now how Joan got confused with the attention from Jim through their sexual encounters as she overly valued his affection. On the surface, for Jim it was a release of stress with a nice girl who made it easy for him. Now this does not excuse Jim from his part in the relationship, but we will discuss that later and show how he reached a point where he only wanted to release stress through sexual encounters.

Almost all of us in one way or another have felt unsure of ourselves, vulnerable or inferior to others. All Joan wanted was acceptance, love and understanding through a committed relationship. So when others would say unusually nice things to her, it appealed to her vulnerable emotional needs for affection and acceptance.

Felicia is another person who was unaware of her internal messages and emotional vulnerabilities, which caused her to ultimately misinterpret one of her co-workers' behaviors in their interactions with each other. Paul was very friendly in the workplace and would go about focusing on his daily responsibilities. Throughout the day he often gave compliments and friendly comments to his co-workers. However, Felicia interpreted his friendliness as flirtatious.

On one occasion she told him that she was going on family leave of absence for a month. Paul told her that he was going to miss her and she viewed his comment as him being fond of her. Felicia further supported her perspective of his fondness when she returned from the leave of absence and Paul expressed that he had missed her pleasant and friendly attitude while she was gone. On another occasion, when a group of co-workers met at a restaurant for lunch, Paul insisted on sitting by his "favorite girl", Felicia.

By now she was convinced that Paul was openly flirting with the intention of them getting together. She began acting on this belief of him liking her and started leaving cards on his office desk. Felicia also positioned herself to have daily encounters with him as she set out to confirm these assumptions. Paul thought her behavior was unusual but still continued his same mannerism of compliments throughout the workplace.

After Paul made no further action towards her impression that he was trying to get with her, Felicia stepped up her game thinking the man was just shy. Calling him at home one evening she invited him to dinner. After speaking with her over the phone, Paul realized that his co-worker was very interested in having a relationship with him. He clarified his friendly attitude as general in the workplace. Felicia was not convinced and had a hunch that he was somehow holding back on his true intentions with her, and after all, he had disclosed that he did not have a girlfriend. Actually, he disclosed that after being questioned. Felicia also thought he was teasing her a bit or wanted to make sure she wanted him.

Upon returning to work the next day, she attempted to confirm her inkling again and sought further confirmation from other co-workers regarding Paul's behavior towards her. They immediately reinforced that his friendliness was general to everyone. In spite of their response, Felicia continued to remain convinced that he somehow had ulterior motives in his friendliness with her. After no further feedback from Paul and observing his friendliness with other co-workers, she began giving him the cold shoulder, making unsavory comments and accused him of being flirty and playing games.

Due to unawareness of her emotional vulnerabilities, Felicia misread Paul's friendly and positive attributes and reported him for harassment. Paul was baffled and very hurt as he realized that his general friendliness had been misunderstood. He was advised by their supervisor to withdraw any further compliments to all in the workplace.

Unfortunately, Felicia made the same erroneous misinterpretations that Joan and most folks do, which was based on her adolescent emotional age which had not been nurtured; the underdeveloped emotions in her adult body automatically misaligned her ability to use solid judgment in her pursuit of a partner. She is not alone in this error as many folks do the same thing and ultimately find themselves in pursuit of others that are not suitable or interested in them. In other words, just like Joan, the pursuit of a fantasy that is not reality is a hot mess as it conflicts with logic. This ultimately rendered Felicia confused with poor judgment where she was passionately mesmerized by someone who had no interest in her. Thank goodness that Paul was a good guy who did not take advantage of her adolescent emotional age causing more injuries to her young emotions.

Now that we know the significance of emotional development to establishing a harmonious inner self without chaos or dissension, it is also important to understand that the parents are not the sole cause of failure to thrive emotionally or bond to others. It would be nice if we could give one grand explanation of what we think contributes to broken relationships, but we know there are many variables in life that may contribute to connecting with others. Our emotional security also gets disturbed and crippled by other disrupting life events and situations including family illness, death and disastrous events in society. Many of these factors usually result in some form of anxiety in our efforts to attach to others, often leading to abandonment and attachment issues. Even an adult may feel somewhat apprehensive to commit to another adult after the death of a spouse. But part of being an adult is accepting the realities of life and coping in a manner that is safe to self and others.

Another outstanding issue is the society we live in often forbids embracing uncomfortable feelings as a whole, consequently leaving many folks with vulnerable emotions. For an example, how many times have you heard little boys being told to stop crying and acting like little girls? They learn to immediately shut down their uncomfortable feelings which occasionally turn into rage at some point inwardly and/or outwardly toward animals, children and wives if not properly addressed. This also prevents them from expressing their total self when trying to align and bond with others. All of us somewhere in time will have moments where things will get to us and when they do, we need to be able to release the related anxiety, however, in a manner that does not hurt us or others.

When we are not allowed to feel hurt and pain from various situations that take place in our lives, it sets us up for failure in our efforts to attach to others. This ultimately results in undeveloped emotions in grown bodies with dysfunctional patterns of transactions in our interactions.

Most of us are looking to do the right things and have a productive life. At times we may feel that our decisions do not work; but at some level they do. We also sometimes base our success and even identity on various things such as having money, a family, a house, a successful career, or a good looking mate with a great body. We look at the lifestyles of the rich and famous and are baffled when they divorce, have legal issues or have a hard time getting along with each other. We even assume that folks who have those things we desire have a better life than we do and are happy and perfect, therefore we are somehow less or not as good. Now it is clear that life can be challenging and things are not always easy, especially living in a world of good and evil.

So how do we address such a pervasive problem that has had such undesired outcomes with so many people from various walks of life? This problem has also destroyed many relationships to include marriages and caused others to avoid committing themselves to long-term relationships.

The reality is that we are all humans; males and females are more alike than different, more so emotionally. Maybe we are fooled by our physical being, blinded, misled, and confused by our own sight.

CAPTURE YOUR THOUGHTS EMOTIONAL VULNERABILITIES

Emotional Survival Games

Now here is the bottom line to *ABCs of Relationships: Emotional Survival Games*. As stated already, emotional responses are learned early on and the primary caregivers get to set the foundation for our emotional life that leads to emotional security or better yet emotional insecurity and threats. We cannot go wrong on this one. When this responsibility is neglected or misguided in any way, our young emotions become stagnated, complex, layered and shelled in our subconscious just waiting for the opportunity to create situations in life that will bring about some form of relief.

I know that is a little deep for some individuals, but the relief is played out through what I refer to as *Emotional Survival Games (ESGs)*. The games are often recognized by our conduct, which is connected to our inner emotional distress that is in need of solace and shaping. Encounters with others are what expose us to that inner distress by triggering old wounds and dredging up all kinds of deeply buried emotions. This ultimately creates a barrier between us and others. However, with self-awareness of the origin of our emotional distress, we are able to change our response patterns and take control of our emotional life while becoming more authentic in our relations with others.

Take Brandon for an example who was incognizant of old thought patterns associated with old emotional wounds in his connections with others. He was recognized in his community as an over achiever because he would go above and beyond to secure success. In spite of a successful career, in his interpersonal relationships Brandon was noticeably unsure of himself and very critical of his own and others' judgments when it appeared that the outcome of a situation would be unfavorable.

He often questioned and sought feedback regarding his own judgment. As a child, Brandon's father would always verbally support his outstanding achievements; however, when he or his siblings were not successful in an endeavor, his father would not make any comments. Brandon did not know what to make of his father's silence given that he was so vocal with favorable outcomes. The young boy ultimately interpreted his father's silence as him <u>not being good enough</u> because somehow he should have known better. Brandon would double his efforts in order to achieve the verbal support from his father. When he became an adult, he tended to reject himself at losses or poor judgment, and ultimately co-workers did not want to work on projects with him.

It was not necessarily the intent of Brandon's father's feedback or lack thereof, but it was the impact that made the difference in Brandon's emotional development. Every word and deed from caregivers is significant in the development of a young child's emotions.

Think about the impact of the following negative statements from a parent to a child. "*How could you be so stupid?*" The child is going to interpret themselves as stupid and then carry it over into adulthood with "*Why do I always pick people who hurt me?*" They torture themselves with an interpretation of being too stupid to pick a partner who will not hurt them. So when others give us feedback or decide to end relationships with us, we become critical of ourselves and often resort to the negative messages regarding the perceptions of our abilities.

We spend endless time scrutinizing assumptions versus being realistic and telling ourselves the truth, which is that no one gets through life unscathed. The point here is that when we do use poor judgment as young children or adolescents, it is an opportunity for our caregivers to help us make the necessary changes in order to avoid the development of repressed and damaging emotional responses. It is also an opportunity for them to teach us problem solving skills and promote confidence in our abilities to achieve, thus producing a healthy self-worth to deal with relationship challenges of all sorts.

As we digress to ESGs, although some of us are motivated and passionate in our quest of inner growth, we sometimes play these games to escape dealing with life on a personal level. We disregard our emotional vulnerabilities and would rather focus on our careers, social status or others.

Because of the lack of emotional guidance early on, we have a tough time putting our true feelings into words. Subsequently we create chaos, drama and deceptive lives along the way while stunting our capacity to grow emotionally and move to a higher functioning of interactions with others and most importantly meet our own goals.

The games will eventually render us the very results we are trying not to get because they are dishonest, superficial in nature and interfere with our true ability to align, bond, and commit to others who may be compatible for us. So how do we recognize *when* we are playing emotional survival games and interacting on the defense in order to interrupt it?

CAPTURE YOUR THOUGHTS EMOTIONAL SURVIVAL GAMES

Characteristics of the Games

As we take a closer look at the games that occur between ourselves and others, they are not always obvious to detect and some are more extreme and dramatic than others. Let me clarify before I go further. I am not saying we are totally ignorant of the games, because I have heard many folks make statements such as *"Stop playing games,"* or refer to a person as *"Just running game..."* There are other comments such as *"She is insecure... a drama queen... so dramatic... trying to get over..."* or *"Stop playing with me."* So there is some suspicion that there is incongruence in our dealings with each other.

When you look at Joan and Jim's relationship and Nina's feedback, she clearly questions Joan's motives and suspected that something was wrong with her. Since Nina was oblivious to emotional survival games, she was left baffled as to why such an accomplished woman would subject herself to a relationship where she was not getting desired results.

I see the games quite a bit in both personal and professional relationships when we are confronted by others. We go into survival mode to protect our reputations and what we think is our dignity. Instead of moving away from the games and presenting our authentic self, we take on a role to relieve whatever emotional distress we are experiencing at the time of the confrontation.

Let's look at these games in more details:

Devaluing

Devaluing includes characteristics such as <u>putting down</u> a person when they do not give us what we want and at the other times <u>idolizing, idealizing or romanticizing</u> when they do give us what we want. Some may refer to that type behavior as borderline. I am just saying, in case you did not know. There is also *name calling*, where people refer to others as crazy, bitches, whores, dogs, bipolar, or using phrases like "*She got problems... Women are devious and evil...*" or "*Oh he is trying to have his cake and ice cream too...*" Yes, when we make these type comments we are actively participating in the games in our own efforts to fill in the blanks of others' motives with us.

Well, if it is starting to stink right now and reading this does not make you feel good, I get it. Those are all toxic and most of all very immature ways of interacting with anyone. When we participate in such games we are suffering from an emotional dilemma that is in need of nourishment and shaping. Recognizing this, in your next interaction before you speak, you may want to pause and check your emotional pulse before responding.

Fix the Past

Fix the Past is another common game often seen in society where we try to ensure events that occurred in childhood do not repeat themselves in our adult relationships. This game is so pervasive that it tends to show up in the work place and intimate relationships as we set up house. This game even leaks over into our parenting so much to the point that we go over and under board trying to spare our children from the emotional distress we suffered in our youth. I hear this game being played when folks say, "*I want my children to have what I did not have and a better life.*" Most parents do the very best that they know how and when they do not, we forgive them and thank God we survived their alleged craziness. Because all parents have a little bit of craziness in their efforts to show how much they love their offspring. As far as the children, they haven't a clue what the parents are trying to fix and ultimately suffer the consequences of being either spoiled, self-centered or basically unprepared for adulthood. As we try to erase our past, we eventually recreate it by replacing parents with spouses and bosses, siblings with co-workers and ourselves with our children. It is beyond a hot mess.

Miriam and Jonathan

Take for example Miriam who married at age nineteen to get away from home. Throughout the first two years of marriage she had a difficult time being responsible, which caused problems with her husband Jonathan. She would spend money, use credit cards impulsively and hang out with her girlfriends until the next morning. She also refused to maintain any household chores in spite of not working while Jonathan worked two jobs to make ends meet. In the past, her partner had voiced his objections only once, however, compromised his objections after Miriam had threatened to divorce him for doing so. The young husband was getting very frustrated given that he wanted to start a family and prepare by saving money.

One day things exploded between the two of them as Jonathan closed out credit cards and later that evening attempted to stop his wife from going out with her friends. Miriam shouted out to him that he was not her father and needed to stop trying to control her. He replied *"Then stop acting like a little girl with no responsibility!"* Before the evening was over, Miriam hit Jonathan and threatened to divorce him again as he attempted to block her from going out. She shouted out *"This is why I got married and left home so that I can get away from my mother who would not let me go out or do things! If this is how you are going to act with me going out, I do not want to have children with you. I do not want them to go through what I did."*

Wait a minute! Did Miriam say that she married Jonathan to go out and do things? Wow, what a great motive to marry;

Mmm, childlike and illogical to the concept of marriage. Marriage is all about responsibility. So she married Jonathan to have the freedom of an adolescent, to go and come with no respect or consideration to her husband or the marriage?

Miriam's upbringing included her parents divorcing when she was ten years old. Her mother had to work two jobs to provide for her and her brother. Miriam had to take on the household responsibilities including babysitting her brother. When she met Jonathan, she was immediately <u>attracted to his soft, gentle, kind, and giving nature</u>. On the other hand, he was <u>attracted to her sense of maturity</u> as he would watch her babysit the younger brother as well as handle household responsibilities. In his mind he was thinking she was the right girl with whom to start a family.

Jonathan's parents had also divorced, yet at a much younger age for him. He was age seven when his father abruptly left his mother. Jonathan was a latch key child who was very afraid when at home alone. He and Miriam shared their pasts with each other and agreed that once married they would stay together forever no matter what would happen between them. They had also agreed that Miriam would stay home and take care of their children.

In spite of similar backgrounds and agreed upon goals to <u>fix their pasts</u>, it is clear that they each had a different image in their minds similar to Joan and Jim, as they went about implementing objectives to meet those goals. What we know for sure is that they both experienced anxiety in their childhoods which was neither guided nor nurtured and ultimately transferred into their marriage.

Miriam had developed an <u>illusory plan</u> of escape to gain freedom from the anxiety associated with her family of origin. She was clearly living on emotional defense in her marriage as she attempted to escape from her childhood experiences. This defensive attitude created chaos and drama in the partnership, which interfered with her ability to function as a responsible adult. Jonathan appeared to have moved past his childhood background as proven by his ability to carry out adult responsibilities. However, his interactions with Miriam and now her threat of divorce re-exposed him to early childhood fears of being alone as well as reminded him of other old wounds that were deeply buried from his own family of origin issues. The problem is that neither Miriam nor Jonathan can <u>fix their pasts</u>.

It is the reality of their childhood and they can not change that script. However, now that they are adults, they can use their family of origin history as a tool to help guide their own relationship while providing themselves new dialogue that will improve their individual emotional lives. The new dialogue will foster emotional liability as they align, bond, and commit themselves to each other, thus producing a better and more compatible relationship.

Well how could the couple recognize that they even had internal dialogues in order to provide new ones?

- ❖ First, they needed to identify <u>their immediate thoughts related to their current events and situations</u>. For an example, Miriam thought that Jonathan was trying to restrict her from new found freedom. Remember when she shouted out, *"That is why I married and left home in order to do things!"* Hence Jonathan thought that he was going to be left alone again.
- ❖ Second, they needed to identify <u>what they were feeling as a result of thinking that freedom was been restricted and abandonment was at hand</u>. They were both feeling anxious and angry.
- ❖ Third, they needed to identify <u>if they had ever felt these feelings before and if so, when and in what situations?</u> Well, their vows to each other are a clear indicator that

their anxieties originated in childhood. Remember, they used marriage as a way out to relieve the angst from their past.

❖ Fourth, <u>how did they react to the threat of abandonment and loss of freedom</u>? Miriam went to the extreme of hitting Jonathan to save her freedom whereas Jonathan tried to prevent abandonment by closing out credit cards and stopping Miriam from going out.

❖ Fifth, <u>what age were the emotional and behavioral responses on their parts?</u> It is clear that Miriam was acting out like a rebellious adolescent. We know that adolescents will act out even in the best family of origin upbringings and want to leave home and do their own things. However, it is the responsibility of the adult caregivers to nurture, support, and properly guide the anxiety that an adolescent/young adult may experience when they feel the urge to leave the nest before they are ready. Now it may appear that Jonathan was acting adult-like as he tried to protect their future; however, his reaction to fear of abandonment limited his ability to align, bond, and connect to his wife in order to generate solutions to their dilemma.

His wife's constant going and staying out late was a trigger that reminded him of lonely and scary events as a young boy and exposed Jonathan to early childhood fears.

Miriam's mother often worked various shifts to make ends meet, which left her in charge throughout the night. Sometimes her mother would abruptly awake her after midnight and whip her for not completing a household chore. Young Miriam also could not hang out with her friends due to having to take care of her younger sibling.

Despite their original goals to remain together no matter what happened between them, as well as their desire for closeness and intimacy, their transactions with each other were dishonest and superficial.

Overall, in spite of their poor motives for marrying (fix the past), their intention was not to end the marriage. Jonathan and Miriam's lack of self awareness regarding the emotional survival games that they were playing was rendering them the very results they were trying not to get.

Theola, Psychiatric Nurse

Theola, a Psychiatric Nurse, was re-exposed to her past first in marriage and again after her divorce as she worked with psychiatric patients on her hospital unit. In retrospect, she realized that she had been raised in a family of origin with an undiagnosed bipolar mother. As Theola encountered many bipolar patients, she recollected that her mother had demonstrated similar mood swings, mania to depression.

As a child she could not understand the mood swings that often resulted in rambling speeches, excessive cleaning and even sometimes aggressiveness during the manic episodes. Her father was very little help as a source of comfort since he complained like a child to the children and appeared helpless to her mother's rapid extremes. He also would often avoid coming home, which left Theola and her siblings alone with their mother during most of her erratic mood swings. Little did her father know that inappropriate things happened in her childhood as a result of his absence, which was also the very trigger to her mother's underlying anxiety.

Divorce was not an option given their religious perspective against it. For Theola, surviving in her family of origin with very little understanding of what was happening to her presented a daily task to the point that she often had nightmares of running away, but even in her dreams her mother would always catch up with her, leaving her desperately hopeless.

Although Theola had several siblings, she often felt alone throughout her childhood. She developed and relied on her survival plan to leave immediately after graduation in order to get away from the environment. Following through with her plans, she went off to college and started the summer semester immediately following graduation, taking courses every semester in order to stay away from home and graduate early.

During her junior year she met Ron who wanted to marry right away. Theola delayed school, married Ron, quickly started their own family and she became a stay at home mom. She had always believed that if she ever had her own family she would have an opportunity to fix her past by doing it the right way. However, Theola did not count on Ron being just as abusive as her mother; he hit her shortly after they were married.

In spite of the abuse, she continued her marriage. As she went about unmindful of the impact of her past, she attempted to rescue her children the same way she needed as a child by overly protecting them. Nevertheless, Theola and Ron's family of origin issues continued to clash. Now she had to figure out how to fix her past while avoiding her husband's abusive behaviors.

Ron's issues started around the age of ten when he went to school one day, returned home to find out that his father had left and another man had moved in all in the same day. Due to his young age, he was unable to understand the dynamics that led to his father's departure. From his perspective his dad left him and allowed his mother to bring in another man.

In his young effort to comprehend what happened, Ron assumed that his mother needed the man for financial support. However, just as he was starting to accept his stepfather, she abruptly uprooted him and his sibling and moved in with another man. Ron was so deeply scared and confused by this that he entered into his own marriage with trust issues and a self-fulfilling prophecy that Theola was going to eventually leave him after she had taken him for everything.

Throughout their marriage he would accuse her of having such motives, which baffled her because in spite of her mother's bipolar behaviors, her parents stayed together. As Ron acted on his self-fulfilling prophecy, he controlled the checkbook to ensure that Theola did not take him for everything and was always in need of him. He often accused her of being too independent; in his eyes needing him meant that she would never abandon him. Ron played the <u>I am going to have some power in how you leave me</u> and the <u>I am the boss of you</u> strategies, as he believed that she could not leave without finances.

After sixteen years of marriage, Theola realized that she was dying on the inside and could neither please Ron nor endure the abusive treatment any longer. She filed for a divorce as she felt responsible for his unhappiness. Theola returned to school and soon became a Psychiatric Nurse. What is sad about this ending is that at the time of the divorce, neither Ron nor Theola had a clue that the emotional distress they experienced in their marriage was due to unresolved emotional dilemmas from their childhood experiences.

CAPTURE YOUR THOUGHTS ABOUT
CHARACTERISTICS OF THE GAMES

Attitudes about Broken Relationships

Relationships today tend to end as rapidly as they start with very little insight gained about the dynamics that occurred within them, the same as Theola and Ron. Ultimately, as we revolve into our next relationship, we transfer all of the same old patterns and behaviors related to unrecognized family of origin entanglements; often with childlike hopes that this is the one that will relieve all of our anxiety experienced in previous unions.

Some of us even believe that with <u>enough time</u> between them we will increase our chances of being more successful. If the truth is told, without the awareness of our emotional status from family of origin issues, time is not even a factor. However, time is a factor if we are doing the inner work that is needed toward that inner emotional growth.

We often make disclaimers after a broken relationship suggesting that <u>it was not meant to be</u>. There is no such thing that a relationship was not meant to be with the exception of those that breed violence. We make these statements as we try to understand and accept our losses. Beyond that, the differences that arise from the exchanges and blows of young emotions, at the end of the day often do exactly what they are suppose to do; which paradoxically will send a message that something is off task in order for us to correct our behaviors and maximize our potential for healthy interactions.

Another disclaimer to failed or poor relationships is often attributed to the "<u>broken picker</u>," which seems to be the modern day explanation of relationships that have ended. How often have you heard individuals ask why it is that they continue to pick the wrong person, or can not seem to pick the right person? Ultimately these folks end up waiting to be picked.

However we resolve in our conscious mind to choose our partner, it is an opportunity to learn parts of ourselves that most of us fear to know or simply do not want to know exist. The feedback that we get from our partners is usually the raw naked truth which, we are spared from the public. All of the tough and difficult challenges we often encounter and experience can help us to find insight that will later serve in future intimate and interpersonal relationships.

CAPTURE YOUR THOUGHTS ABOUT BROKEN RELATIONSHIPS

Development of Self-Distorted Themes

Not Good Enough

Sometimes the interruption of emotional development may be as innocent as Kevin who at age seven lost his father to death. His mother who was preoccupied with her own grief <u>did not properly nurture and guide Kevin's confused emotions</u>. Because he did not get the proper emotional guidance from an adult caregiver, he later transferred this experience of loss into issues of abandonment and attachment. Due to his lack of understanding regarding the absence of his father, he developed a fantasy that his father would soon return.

Kevin <u>needed emotional guidance</u> and reassurance that it was okay to experience the uncomfortable feelings he did in the realization of his father's absence. Kevin's emotions became stunted as a result of the unfulfilled fantasy. His mother later re-married however, and shortly afterward divorced; his stepfather blamed him for his departure.

The combination of the two losses ultimately contributed to distorted relationship themes as Kevin attempted to bond with others. His self-distortions included faulty thinking like:

- ❖ Not being able to keep someone in his life
- ❖ Not being good enough for others to stay around
- ❖ It is his fault when others choose to end the relationship

We have all heard these and other distorted themes and even supported them in our own efforts to understand what went wrong, especially since things started out so great. As an adult, in spite of Kevin's desire to have a relationship, he would end relationships as soon as he would get close to an individual due to his fear that it would not last anyway.

It is obvious that Kevin played the <u>avoid losses</u> emotional survival game with the <u>pull and push</u> strategy, in order to avoid painful emotional experiences of separation. This ultimately left a mud path that he continued to track into new relationships.

Staying/Hoping/Wishing/Compromising

Some of us tend to go to the opposite extreme of Kevin by playing a <u>staying/hoping/wishing game</u> where we stay in spite of the poorness of a relationship in order to prove that <u>we are good enough</u> or to <u>avoid loneliness</u>. Often when courting we are too focused on the <u>need to commit or not commit</u> versus getting to know each other by learning similar values, thought patterns, beliefs and expectations. Does this scenario sound familiar? Well I will say one word, Joan.

Joan

Joan convinced herself that <u>if she was good enough</u> then Jim would commit. She will be so good to him that he will never leave her and she will not be alone. Inevitably when he did not respond as such, she told herself that she obviously was <u>not good enough</u> and ultimately would end up alone; at least that is what she thought in her efforts to fill in the blanks. What made their interactions dishonest on her part was her <u>desperation to not be alone</u>, which resulted in her trying to match herself with someone who was not ready for a committed relationship. Ultimately she avoided taking stands and put up with all types of crap, inconsideration, and rudeness in hopes that her lover would stay and not leave her the same as her parents. She <u>compromised</u> everything and then would get upset when she did not get the expected payoff in spite of her sacrifices. It took Joan going to therapy to realize that she was in a revolving door type of relationship where Jim was in and out.

The flip side of this interaction is that when people do stay, we lose respect for them and begin the devaluing game. It would seem logical that once we get the person to stay, we turn into real people again, which parallels the romantic crap of "*Oh, I love the way they brush their teeth,*" then flip flops to "*I cannot stand the way they brush their teeth.*" Then it shifts into the discovery game of "*Who are you really?*" or "*I do not even know you,*" which is so predictably followed by "*Oh my god, what was I thinking? You lied to me. You told me this (or that).*" The danger involved with this staying game is that often times we find ourselves with a belief system that if we finally get it right, then we are good enough to live. This often gets interpreted into we should die if we are not good enough, which is the ultimate abandonment of the child. People who play the staying game believe that others are the key to their lives and when they are not good enough, they often go to that very sad place of depression, suicidal ideation, isolation, and loneliness.

Mason & Norma

Well, let's look at a staying game on Mason and Norma's part, each of whom were divorced about the same time and had been married for about eighteen years. They met at a social event. Mason claimed that he was not looking for a relationship (the same as Jim), however aggressively pursued Norma who was only minimally interested in him. They went to dinner a couple of times and Mason remained aloof in his unavailability in spite of his pursuit of Norma. She was okay with this given her minimal interest in him anyway.

On one quiet Saturday afternoon, Mason proposed a more casual less expensive outing at the last minute since neither of them had anything to do. He suggested that Norma come over to his place to watch a movie and later go to dinner afterwards. Prior to Norma's arrival, boundaries were discussed and she was very clear that there would be no hanky panky; of course, Mason agreed. However, during the movie he became very sexually assertive in his efforts toward hanky panky. Norma became confused about how to respond to his efforts, however giggled and joked and the two engaged sexually.

She unknowingly had regressed to a younger emotional state of early childhood abuse as she engaged sexually with Mason. After all, this interaction was familiar to her where boundaries had been crossed and trust was broken. She trusted Mason and now that it had been broken, she felt responsible. Because after all it was her fault as she could hear her grandmother saying, *"What did you think a man wanted by inviting you to his apartment?"* This implying how stupid she was to believe that a man would want her for anything else.

Norma could also hear her stepfather saying by his past incestuous actions that *"This is what women are to do."* Norma had developed a script from child hood believing the world had not ever wanted her, which she supported with her mother's negative abusive attention and the absence of her father. From her perspective, her siblings were adored as evidenced by the positive attention they received.

Therefore, the message that young Norma interpreted regarding her self-worth was that she was a bother or in the way, which she transferred into her adult interactions with others, leaving many of her friends baffled. Moreover, as she regressed in her thinking, she began to blame herself for being in this situation. Rather than pushing Mason off in the first place and leaving his apartment, she began a relationship with him, partly to prove that she was not a victim.

After all he was a good man, he did not actually rape her and she never yelled "no!" Then why did it feel so bad and not fun to Norma? Well, Norma and Mason discussed the event later, in which Mason shared that he had not planned or prepared for the sexual encounter either. As Norma reflected on her responses that evening, how could Mason have known that she was uncomfortable, unwilling and in emotional distress given that she did not protest but rather giggled and made jokes.

Later she tried to break off the relationship by refusing to answer the phone when he would call. However, she finally answered the phone and told him she no longer wanted to see him. As she struggled with her logic and emotions regarding her self worth, in spite of her attempt to break up with Mason and his continuous pursuit, she gave in and began a sexual relationship with him. Part of her reasoning was that he did not seem to be a callous man given that he was educated and loved his family a lot. This man was adored and respected by others; so why should she not take the chance?

Now the staying game began where she set out to prove that she was not a whore or victim and that she could keep a man. Also, what was going on with Mason who did not want a relationship by his report, but agreed to a monogamist sexual relationship with her? What drove Norma crazy was that he did and did not want her and he did and did not love her. Sounds familiar.

We know that in Norma's family of origin, incest occurred and she entered into relationships with childlike hope that maybe this is the one after all. She began to idealize Mason by focusing only on his positive qualities and characteristics. Remember Joan who associated positive verbiage to her inner self-worth? It appealed to her emotional vulnerabilities. Now with Mason, it may appear that he was clear in his communication regarding not wanting a relationship. His family of origin history was similar to Kevin's where his father passed when he was age nine, and it would seem impossible that he would not have an exaggerated experience of loss.

Is it possible that Mason could have created a dialogue of "*I cannot let myself go,*" the same as Kevin? "*If I allow myself to love and commit to a woman, she may go away, the same as my father. If I do not love her that much then I do not have that much to lose and we could just get our physical needs met.*" Could this dialogue have somehow been reinforced by the dynamics in his past marriage as well as other incomplete relationships?

Great Friendship/No Relationship/But Benefits

Wow. Norma and Mason's interaction is similar to that of Jim and Joan. Let's compare the two relationships. Both Jim and Mason wanted to play the Great Friendship / no relationship game, naively unaware of their underlying fears of commitment and abandonment. In this game usually, one partner wants sex with no attachment and the other generally wants attachment. The plan usually sounds like "*We will get together when it is convenient for us both, have fun, satisfy each others' needs and go out and do things.*" It sounds pretty fair.

In this agreement, each partner supposedly has their own life. However, in actuality it is not when both are able to get together. It is usually on the time table of one partner only. Here is what we know about Jim: He was a very successful individual career wise who had married and divorced twice. Jim came from a family of origin where his father was a politician and everything on the surface with his parents appeared very normal. However, behind the scenes his parents fought a lot as his father was also a womanizer and his mother drank heavily to cope with his infidelity.

Jim and his siblings often shouldered the brunt of their parents' anger toward each other. From early on Jim had decided he would not marry. However in spite of this disclaimer, he married his first wife at age eighteen due to pregnancy and his parents urged him to do "the right thing." That marriage was short lived. After only one year, Jim learned that his wife was having an affair with an ex-boyfriend. In spite of his efforts to forgive her and continue the relationship, his wife continued the affair. After learning that the ex-boyfriend was the biological father of their child, Jim finally divorced her.

He married his second wife due to feeling sorry for her son whose father was absent from his life. That relationship ended after three years. When he met Joan, he was very attracted to her. Though by that time, his fear of commitment was active and full blown to the point that he was unable to commit even to a date. This often left Joan confused but happy to hear from him and relieved that he had not moved on.

The original agreement of convenience for both was only fair to Jim. As far as Joan was concerned, waiting for the phone to ring felt like a lack of connection, friendship and a relationship. The level of friendship was negotiated on an ongoing basis. She felt that somehow staying with Jim and not moving on seemed to validate some form of relationship, since the idea of moving on suggested some form of loose behavior, unfaithfulness or the inability to hang in there.

The similarity between all four individuals is that they were all playing the same emotional survival game in their own way as they struggled and suffered with fear of attachment and ultimately abandonment. The ultimate fear for Jim and Mason was, "If I let go and let myself love, then the other person will leave me and I will be abandoned and abandonment means that I will die." The ultimate fear for Norma and Joan was nearly the same that "If I let go, then there will be no one else and I will be totally alone and I will die."

Sometimes this game is played inside of marriages where one partner feels like the other is going to leave them and of course wants to be the first partner in charge of when and how their spouse will do so. Abandonment is an issue of infancy; without the proper intervention an infant will die of abandonment.

The cycle of sabotaging and non-committal behaviors continues on until one partner decides that they have had enough and changes partners, beginning the cycle again. Usually the change is motivated by some superficial external package or the hope that this plan will work with someone else that is not so needy. The partner that suggested the break-up usually sees themselves as okay. Both Mason and Jim would do just enough to keep Norma and Joan engaged and involved in their idea of friendship, which was enough for Norma and Joan to love them but little hope for a future together.

Jim and Mason would randomly call or see Joan and Norma, but if any predictability was noted or pointed out they would change their routine of interactions, not wanting to be tied down to any form of commitment. All parties were interacting in an illusory manner with confused emotions, which greatly clouded their judgment in their relations with each other.

In Joan and Norma's illusion, it would appear that Jim and Mason would give just a little bit more of themselves each time, which contributed to false hope that the relationship had a long-term future. But if Jim and Mason sensed giving any part of themselves they both would bristle and decrease their interactions with Norma and Joan, in quality and quantity. Given that neither Mason nor Jim would take the relationships any further due to fear of commitment, Norma and Joan compromised their own standards, values and judgments by trying to participate in the special friendship game without strings or attachment.

After playing this game for about a year, Mason announced that he wanted to go out with an old female friend from high school, which led to a discussion with Norma of monogamy and if kissing the old friend would be okay. From this conversation, Mason told Norma that they could remain friends because he did not want to hurt her. Norma interpreted his response as hypocritical to his personal values. Norma also noticed a pattern of one year relationships in Mason's past that ended as those partners announced their desire to marry him.

If we should take a closer look at Mason and his own version of previous relationships, it is clear that he played the emotional survival game by avoiding letting his feelings develop for a woman. His need for emotional safety from being hurt was so powerful that he was unable to let himself love or be loved. Let's look at some of the controlling elements on his part in this emotional survival game.

Throughout the one year period of Mason and Norma's situationship, they would spend time together that was very intimate, caring and warm. Then they would have periods of no contact at all and Norma would feel as if Mason had fallen off the face of the earth. The cycle would repeat itself and it appeared that the closer they would get to each other, the longer the no contact periods would be on Mason's part. He would tell Norma that it was okay for her to call but when she did call he was clearly unavailable and very cold, which she interpreted as rejection and responded with very hurt feelings. This further strengthened his <u>control of detachment</u>.

After one of those periods of detachment, Mason called Norma and scolded her for not calling him; this baffled her. She had finally reached a point where she was able to tell him that she could not "just kind of love" him and be there at his convenience. Furthermore, Norma's needs did not seem to matter on Mason's part being that he was unwilling and unable to meet them. Unwilling in that he needed to <u>control the closeness</u> between them. Unable because he was <u>unaware in order to change it</u>. Despite Norma's resolve, Mason still calls her to this day and Norma still receives his phone calls and occasional invitations to visit. Joan and Norma saw themselves as victims in their interactions with Jim and Mason.

Control the Closeness

Now there are others who would respond quite differently to Jim and Mason. Take Lana who was a savvy and brazen dater and had dated Jim briefly. Jim offered her the same <u>Great friendship game</u> as he had offered Joan. However, when Lana recognized that Jim was trying to <u>control the closeness</u> between them, of course being the game changer that she was, played the <u>tit for tat game</u> and reversed the control. Jim, naively thinking that he was still in control of their interaction, expressed concerns of lovers getting caught up in the friendship and wanting more. Lana brazenly told Jim that she sure hoped he would not have that problem because that would really interfere with their good friendship.

Lana was clear about her intention in dating and adjusted her interaction by eliminating sexual encounters with him. This left Jim baffled and unsure of how to deal with her. He eventually stopped calling Lana when he realized that he was not able to play the same game with her as with Joan; recognizing that he was no longer in control.

The difference between Joan and Lana is that Joan was interacting in the relationship with Jim like a young girl hoping and wishing he would eventually stay and commit to her the way she had hoped her parents would stay home. Joan's family of origin included her parents fighting so much that one parent or the other would abruptly leave the home for long periods of time. She would go on her best behavior and often times begged and pleaded with her parents to not leave. Joan, who was now thirty seven and had already experienced several broken relationships, was now hoping that Jim was the one to relieve her of all the past relationship pain.

Cornelia

Perhaps you did not see yourself or anyone you know in the previous emotional survival games where folks developed self-distorted themes that ultimately become barriers in their relationships. So, let's take a quick glance at an emotional survival game where society and culture are huge factors and folks try to rid their pasts by breaking through the glass ceilings of social, economic and gender roles.

Cornelia, a baby boomer, played an emotional survival game to cope with past hurtful childhood memories. She is a beautiful sixty-five year old Hispanic woman who despite her beauty, charm and intelligence, has been alone most of her life. She shared that in her younger days she was quite beautiful and had many admirers. Cornelia married once but divorced her husband because he was not good enough for her. Many men approached her but she considered them as not good enough for her; meanwhile she approach men of a higher social and economic classes to include Doctors, Lawyers and well off Businessmen. She also engaged in affairs with wealthy married men.

In Cornelia's self-reflection of interactions with these men, she realized that because she thought she was too good for them, she now was alone and longed to have a companion. She shared her regrets and hopes of spending her last days with a companion. Although it may appear that Cornelia was too conceited for her own good, she was actually hiding her negative thoughts and feelings about herself, which is evident in the outcome of her life.

After getting to know Cornelia and her family of origin history, it became easier to understand why she sought out wealthy men. Shortly following the death of her father, Cornelia's mother worked for a well to do White family. Due to the unavailability of extended family members, Cornelia lived with her mother in the back of this family's home. Being pretty, she was well liked and allowed to play with the children in the family as well as their neighbors. However at more public activities such as birthday parties, she was not allowed to join, which she interpreted as not being good enough innately.

Despite obvious reasons for personal and family worth, being that her father died fighting for the country and the mother worked hard at supporting the family, Cornelia lacked emotional support to counteract the negative messages experienced in this environment. As a result, she transferred this script into her adult interactions as she tried to fix this not good enough feeling. To this day Cornelia still lives alone with many regrets of not getting the results she desired.

CAPTURE YOUR THOUGHTS ABOUT THE STAYING/HOPING/WISHING/COMPROMSING GAMES

The Exchange Station

My Knight in Shining Armor

The exchange station is where we meet folks to exchange information in order to rule in or out if someone is compatible for us. This trade of information is critical to making the best choice for our future. The problem that generally occurs at the exchange station is faulty expectations and demand, which most people error hugely and find themselves in unhealthy situations or relationships. The goal is that we are prepared to use good judgment which will not compromise our values and self-worth in our effort to connect to others. We often meet others at a crossroad along our path or opposite direction the same as Vinya who met Arthur while completing her junior and senior year in college. Perhaps she was already looking to meet someone along this path in hopes that they were going in the same direction.

Vinya prayed to meet a young man with integrity and good character. When she met Arthur, it seemed her prayers had been answered as she'd dreamt of someone with similar characteristics. Here are those feel good signals again from chapter three which we associate to our inner self-worth that made us feel strongly compelled to go toward the other person. As we tell Vinya's story, we will answer the question on if she became distracted by external signals and diverted from her path and plans in an effort not to lose the liberator whom she believed would meet her needs.

Our awareness and sensitivities to our vulnerabilities will help us to not misinterpret or assign illusive values to those signals. When Vinya met Arthur she was on the rebound and mad at another young man, so meeting him was refreshing as they exchanged similar values and were able to appreciate each other's cultures. She enjoyed their contact so much at their first meeting that she did not want it to end and ultimately spent the evening with him instead of returning to her dorm room.

At the exchange station, some of us swap enough information and agree to continue the process while the rest of us get stuck and begin compromising by altering our plans and values to assimilate the other person's path, plans and values. As time passed between Vinya and Arthur, adjustments were made to their values and it appeared as if they had settled. But somehow along the way Vinya's plans became more and more altered as she adjusted her own to accommodate Arthur's plan into their future. It now appeared that his plan was the only one to nurture because hers had been revised and manipulated.

Vinya was now starting to feel the impact of what she had done and realized that the more her plans were transformed to secure the relationship, the farther away she was from her original goals.

The Epiphany of Vinya

After five and a half years of holding on to the relationship with Arthur and two months apart from him, Vinya decided that it was no longer worth it. Over the course of the five years, Arthur had dumped her at least three to five times. To Vinya it seemed as if he had dumped her for every year they had been together.

As she reflected on her reasons for staying in the relationship, she realized that she'd been in denial of reality regarding the various dynamics which had occurred throughout. Arthur communicated at various times that they were going in two different directions. When he relocated to complete his educational goals, Vinya followed and set up house for the two of them. Arthur told her on several occasions that she should not have followed him. He told her that he needed the time apart.

At that time, Vinya thought she could not handle a long distance relationship as she believed it would not survive. Part of what kept her desperately holding on to Arthur was that they had been together for five and a half years and were each other's first in the sharing of their innocence which meant something to her. After all he had not cheated or been physically abusive to her or lapsed into drugs of any sort. She further justified her staying by thinking that she would never find those qualities in anyone else. However, when she looked at her current male friends, she realized that they all had those same qualities.

Material and financial investments made on her part throughout the relationship also contributed to her hanging in there as long as she did. Not only that, Vinya was still obligated several more months for the apartment she had rented for the two of them as he was unable to maintain it on his own. As far as she was concerned, their parting of ways was going to be the same as a divorce.

Vinya also realized that Arthur's own unhappiness was cutting into their relationship as he would compliment her along with an insult. He would often tell her that she was pretty but needed to tone up various parts of her body. At other times in her effort to give him constructive feedback, he would accuse her of being negative and attacking him. No matter what she did somehow she did not meet his expectations.

As Vinya Struggled with her investments and decision to move on she could not help but to reflect on Arthur not having many friends or current financial means to support him self while completing his Bachelor's degree. His vocational and occupational goals were worth supporting given that he was the first in his family to graduate from high school and earned an Associate's degree. She knew that Arthur really wanted to achieve, however, simply lacked the motivation to assertively pursue his goals. She was tired and realized that she could no longer keep up the facade that things were going to lead into marriage.

When she looked closer at Arthur's behaviors throughout the five years, she realized that all of her supported efforts to help him meet his personal goals were placing her self-worth at risk if she continued to hold on at this time. Although she had told herself that she would never try to change a man, she thought Arthur would at least appreciate a little support and help as he struggled to complete his educational goals. Vinya would often get annoyed watching him lay in bed and miss three consecutive days from school as her upbringing was to go to school, make A's and B's, then move on and do something with your life. So being a decent citizen, she thought why not support him in his efforts. She realized that in all of her efforts, she had isolated herself in hopes of marriage and security in his life. Now that she had moved away and made contact with old friends, she no longer felt as isolated and did not need to cling on to someone because they were there. Vinya concluded that if they were meant to have a life together long-term that somehow it would work itself out.

As she talked with various friends, both male and female, she realized her level of maturity and decided that she would like to interact with someone on a more mature level. Mature in what way? Given that Arthur's family of origin contained marital difficulties between his parents, we can safely say that he may have unknowingly projected some of his own insecurities about long-term commitment into their relationship.

But what was Vinya's emotional vulnerability and internal dialogue that really perpetuated her subjection to verbal comments that slowly devoured away at her self-worth? Her original plans to remain a virgin prior to marriage had been compromised and altered, which she attributed to her realization and low probability of finding a virgin when she was ready to marry; since Arthur had been a virgin, she was willing to take the risk and compromise her value no matter the outcome. However, her emotional vulnerability started at a very early age when her mother told her to stop acting ugly. Vinya interpreted this comment into her mother referring to her as ugly.

Also at the age of twelve her mother divorced her father and left the home. In spite of being aware of problems between her mother and father, she had a difficult time understanding the divorce. She blamed her mother for breaking up their family. From these events Vinya developed a low self-worth identity that she ultimately transferred into her adult relationships.

Here is where we have the chaos. She met Arthur at a crossroad, which we will call the exchange station. The exchange station is where we learn about others. It is just that and that alone. We learn things about the other person as we interact with them. We need that exchange of communication and interaction in order to make long-term decisions with the other person. In this case, Vinya was very young and somewhat naïve about relationships as most folks are at that age.

Meet My Demands

One of the most common games, played at the exchange station is the, <u>meet my demands to prove you want to be with me</u>. This game is where folks initially tend to utilize the time talking about all the things that went wrong in their last relationships, which is no more than a subtle way of laying out their demands for a self-centered relationship. The more the person's appearance meets society expectations of good looks, the potential partner tends to fall for this ploy, especially when they are unaware about their emotional vulnerabilities. If they move forward from this conversation, it is all a superficial exchange from that point. On the surface it may not appear as such but it is no different than a two year old in a grocery store being demanding with a parent. This game usually sounds like, *"If we are going to be together, you are going to have to do this, this and that."* And when the person does not, a temper tantrum is thrown to call in the demands. Then they run and tell their friends that the person gave them flowers, a ring, or cooks for them, does their laundry and swings on a pole. They foolishly set out to <u>prove their worth</u> through the potential partner's compliance to their demands all while parading around gifts collected from this new partner, aka the emotionally vulnerable pushover (*EVP*). Generally their friends respond with, *"It must be good, you have it going on."*

Wow, so misaligned! What are we doing? Everyone at this exchange station was in the moment of their excitement, the attraction and whim. Now when the love dust settles down, we begin devaluing them with our poor judgment of what we thought they were. Remember in chapter seven that flip flop to *"I cannot stand the way they brush their teeth"* where we shift into <u>the discovery game</u> of *"Who are you really"* or *"I do not even know you."* Life is teaching us that a microwave exchange with the expectation of a long-term relationship does not work. We have to put in the work that is required to get lasting results like some of our parents.

Faulty Expectations: Me, Me and Mine

Another common game that goes off task at the exchange station is that *Faulty expectations list*. It is similar to the *Meet My Demands* game but is played more subtly, sometimes even in a passive aggressive manner; Meaning upfront they never put the expectation out there but when the potential mate fails to present, then there is that lashing of the tongue about what the person does not do for them. The subtle attitude usually goes something like, *"You did not get me anything for my birthday, I thought you loved me."* Some men tend to talk just as confused, *"You don't cook, scratch my back, clean or wash my clothes."* Wow, what a bond and web we have weaved as we are unhealthily socialized in our effort to bond with others.

Slowing down must be a priority when we meet people and try to align with them. We have to learn more about the person of interest that we feel so excited about. Slow down! Learn as much information as possible and enjoy the exchange before ripping yourself apart with relationship drama and suicide with assumptions. Half of our decisions to get together are based on fantasies and the other half on unrealistic expectations. You may say what is the difference? There is always the possibility for a fantasy to occur but realistically it will not. Apart from that you need to know who you are inside first (especially your emotional vulnerabilities), before you can truly have a genuine and healthy exchange with others as well as increase your chances of being successful in relationships.

It is okay to put our values and standards on the table in spite of the loss we think we will experience. It gives us an opportunity to see how the potential partner will compare. That is the whole point. At the exchange station, we have nothing to lose because there is no obligation or commitment. If along the way we decide we are not willing to do a long-term relationship with the other person, then communicate it clearly and move on. At the very least, maybe you can develop a long-term friendship from the genuine exchange. The bottom line is that when we are dishonest and superficial with all the faulty expectations, guess what? We learn the hard way with regrets about our judgment and ultimately do not get the results we are trying to get.

CAPTURE YOUR THOUGHTS ABOUT THE EXCHANGE STATION GAMES

Marital Games

As we exit our family of origin and start our own families, some of us work very hard on the surface trying to present our marriages as perfect and loving. However, when it falls down to our ankles as we have been re-exposed to our family of origin issues, we have no place to go but to tell the truth as we feel that we are going to lose it. We try our best to honor and hang on to our commitments as we believe this is what we should do.

Until Death Do Us Part

As Jamie reflected on twenty-nine years of marriage to Donald, she felt as if she had walked into a huge spider web that felt slimy and sticky with twisted strands of yarn. She felt betrayed, frustrated, confused, alone and certainly not loved by Donald. Her upbringing taught her that marriage was about happiness and fulfilling until death separated the two of them. But for the most part, as far as Jamie was concerned, death had taken a detour and was no where near.

As she tried to understand the entrapped and entangled feelings, information from her upbringing only brought about a silent scream because surely she was not supposed to discuss her thoughts and feelings about her marriage outwardly. Jamie felt as if she was drowning in a vast sea of emptiness as she struggled with her frustration of trying to cling to the traditions of marriage the way she understood it. She had reached a point of disenchantment.

The counseling received from church leaders was to hang on and "God" was going to send deliverance. What! Deliverance? Wait a minute, at the inception of the marriage she heard *"Until death do us part"* and *"No written divorce"*; but now a third D, *"Deliverance!"* So as she waited on deliverance, she tried to make sense of this thing called marriage by going to therapy and reading self-help books.

As the disenchanted wife listened to Therapists or turned the pages of the books, she tried to grab hold of any glimpse of light that would shine and incorporate any tools that would spark life into their union. In the self help books she found that the Sixties placed great emphasis on the role of the husband as the head and provider of the marriage, while the wife was the weaker of the two and the children's caretaker. The Seventies offered emphasis on lack and need of communication, which cracked the doors to the idea of understanding and respect of the individual apart from the various roles in marriage. The Eighties brought aboard liberation and caused a rift in the tradition of marriage as a whole. By the early Nineties, divorce was the norm as adultery was rampant with the freedom of sexuality. Some spouses began coming out of "the closet," while others abandoned the concept that two shall become one and invited others into their bedrooms, commonly known as "swinging." By the millennium, marriage was hardly a word of honor as couples rotated from house to house trying to get the mate on the "greener" side of the pasture.

It is interesting that Jamie used a spider web to describe the entanglement and entrapment she felt about her partnership with Donald. As far as she was concerned, her marriage did not function as a union the same as a spider with two main divisions. She definitely did not feel enough support as she pushed and pulled throughout the entire relationship to get decent shelter and security for their family.

Jamie and her husband both had formal degrees. She had leadership responsibilities in her job and Donald owned his business. It would seem logical that these two individuals should be able to manage their marriage with some degree of success. Throughout the years, they both were highly critical of each other including verbal and occasional physical aggression.

The aligning, bonding, and commitment that occur within a relationship will depend on the emotional age of the two individuals. From Jamie's perspective, she was the only adult in the relationship as Donald was on a mission to prove that he and he alone was going to run his world. At one point Jamie decided that since she could not divorce Donald she would at least live separate from him.

Donald rose to the occasion and went above and beyond to secure the marriage. He did everything that she requested of him and then some. He went to counseling, pursued her romantically and decided it was time to get a new house. Jamie was shocked but embraced her husband's efforts and put aside the separation as she believed that the deliverance had arrived.

As they attempted to improve their marriage, they slowly began to regress to old patterns of interacting with each other and Jamie slowly began to realize the web that had been weaved. Given Donald's first response at their separation, she would remind and threaten him with another one. Contradictory to his behavior within the marriage, he would rise to the occasion and interrupt her departure. Jamie would feel satisfied as her separation deliverance speech would make its mark. Wow, what type of emotional survival game were these two playing? Logically, Jamie and Donald both could provide for themselves, so staying together was not about getting basic needs met.

For Jamie, it appears that she was trying to secure her spiritual vows by not divorcing Donald. Okay, then what was the problem? She agreed to stick it out with this guy for better or worse. Did she not understand her own vows or was her commitment childlike in hopes that her spouse would be absent of the worst? What about Donald? What kept him in a marriage for so many years where he fought vehemently to do whatever he wanted to do without much consideration to his wife, yet contradictorily go above and beyond to secure it at the threat of divorce?

Jamie and Donald played the "I am going to leave you" versus "I do not want to be alone game." So let's look a little closer into elements that each of them brought into the marriage from their family of origin. Was Jamie overlooking something apart from her vows to avoid divorcing Donald and projected something from her family of origin unknowingly? Throughout the marriage Jamie compromised voicing her thoughts, as she had learned in her family of origin that a wife was to keep quiet because the husband was the head. Internally she would fill up with anxiety and was unable to express herself about various issues; this led to outbursts on her part from time to time.

The content of those outbursts exposed Donald to insecurities and deficiencies on his part, which he was already aware of and did not want to hear about them from his wife. He had felt this way throughout childhood and adolescent years as his peers would tease him and his siblings. Donald grew up in a poorly developed community and an environment of domestic violence on the part of his father until his parents divorced. Because Donald was his father's favorite child he often felt guilty and powerless in the situation, going back and forth between both parents' homes. He pledged to educate himself in order to have a nice decent home and family. In spite of his desire to have a family and motive to fix his past, he sabotaged his own desire as he tried to recapture the power he lacked as a young boy.

Not Good Enough

Some individuals find themselves feeling resentful towards their mates and will begin sabotaging their marriages due to low self-worth and confidence. This is exactly what happened to Spencer who was very sarcastic with his wife Susan in public. His wife was very beautiful with a well kept body while he was out of shape. Though Spencer's wife had chosen him over another man, his own insecurities led him to act out a series of sabotaging behaviors in their marriage due to his fears that she would eventually leave him.

Now Spencer, the same as all the others, was not aware that he had transferred unresolved family of origin issues into his relationship. He was born out of wedlock and raised by a lady in the neighborhood from the age of twelve after his mother did not return from one of her drug binges. His parents were both addicts and eventually ended in prison. The young boy developed a distorted dialogue that somehow he was *responsible for his parents' absence* due to *not being good enough*. Therefore, *"If my own parents did not want me why should Susan want me, especially since I am so out of shape? My own mother left, so eventually my wife will leave and I want to be in charge of when and how she leaves."* What about Spencer's wife? Why did she tolerate the ongoing verbal abuse from him? Well, her family of origin was very traditional: stay together no matter what happens.

There are other times in marriages where couples play very vicious games as they try to relieve emotional distress. The <u>stand off</u> game is where one partner is holding the other partner emotionally hostage by distant, withdrawn and passive aggressive responses. The other partner usually takes the aggressive stance with argumentative and sometimes physically aggressive responses. It may appear that the passive partner is less noxious in their response; however both are making an outcry of emotional distress as evidenced by them remaining in the relationship.

Power Struggle

It would seem logical that if someone is unhappy with their partner they would work on resolutions to improve the relationship or simply move on. But somehow people have a difficult time making the decision to remove themselves from what they think is making them unhappy. This game also contains an element of *power struggle* as each member is determined to get the response that they want from their partner.

Melinda was so happy when she met Moose that she wanted to marry him right away. However, he was not ready to marry. He treated her wonderfully as he held the power to their union in his hand. After seven years of holding out on Melinda, Moose finally asked her to marry him. They married and shortly afterwards he became very critical of his wife. She tolerated as much as she could but would separate from him from time to time in an effort to maintain her sanity. Melinda started feeling as if Moose was trying to take away her identity. As she became more distant and withdrawn with passive aggressive responses, he became even more critical, argumentative and verbally aggressive.

What kept these two together was their strong need to *prove their stance* as they both power struggled to stay in the relationship. Melinda wanted to prove that her husband would not take away her identity while Moose was trying to prove that he could do something right. After all, it was his third marriage. Maintaining her identity was important to Melinda as she had struggled for it since childhood. In her family of origin, she had not known her birth mother or father as she was raised in foster care. She had struggled for years over this issue and prior to meeting Moose, had reached a content place in life where she was able to accept her past without feeling that _something was wrong with her_. Moose's family of origin contained much criticism where he felt as if he could never meet his parents' expectations of him. After two divorces he was out to _prove that he could succeed at something_ and Melinda was it. Though instead of being genuine with his true feelings, he dug his heel in and functioned on a faulty theme that he could not do anything right.

Ultimately, Moose and Melinda both struggled with their self-worth and blamed each other for their unhappiness; they were mean, nasty and did not want to remain in the union. Occasionally Melinda would even go as far as suggesting that Moose would do her a favor by just leaving.

The question with this couple is what was keeping them in the marriage in spite of its desolation? They both had a choice to either improve the relationship or simply leave. In this case, they both were trying to confirm their self-worth and played the fix our mate game by trying to correct each other's shortcomings. In truth, it is not our job to fix our mates but our role is to work on ourselves; the most we can do for them is recognize when they are in distress and provide support. As we improve our own imperfections, hopefully our mates will recognize their personal errors and begin correcting them proactively. We have the choice to either participate in our partner's issues or work around them without becoming whiners, complainers and or fixers.

Peace Sake, Secure the Marriage

Another pervasive marital ESG is the peace sake game to avoid emotional anguish by going along with their mate in spite of taking a stand. No one wins in this game and surely the _relationship will not thrive_ as the interaction is phony. As a matter of fact, this game definitely creates a barrier between partners.

Another marital ESG we tend to play out of fear of abandonment is the secure the marriage by acting out using the I am in charge strategy as we feel we have to be completely in control, the same as Ron did with Theola. We set up our relationships to control our mates by telling them what they can and cannot do. The more they comply with our demands and wishes, the more we believe we're in charge of their staying with us and do not have to worry about them leaving. This sends our emotional vulnerabilities a message that we are needed and if we are needed then we will not be alone. Sometimes we go to such extremes as playing on their vulnerabilities as we bully or threaten to harm ourselves to manipulate them to stay. Other times we throw temper tantrums, pout, and withdraw. What is sad about this game and stance is that we are very angry and frustrated on the inside.

Ultimately, we end up defeating ourselves and sabotaging the relationship due to our own misery which we have projected onto our mate. Furthermore, sometimes when our partner is the in charge mate, we go against our own values and standards as we subject ourselves to their ill-behaviors out of fear and the intimidation of losing them in our lives. When we play the do not leave me game at this level, we are vulnerable to slipping into their control. As we are bewildered with our own sense of powerlessness, we want to make sure that the controller is not upset with us or what we do; this tends to foster us losing our own thinking and freewill. We also tend to become very miserable and sometimes even suicidal as we feel responsible for the controller's actions.

Finally, we sometimes attempt to validate our self-importance by holding others accountable through idealized expectations of what we believe they should have done for us. We suggest that if they loved or cared about us they would not have forgotten our birthday or anniversary. We even go as far as to say that they would have bought us gifts or taken us to special places if they truly loved or cared about us. Whether we play this game with our mates, friends or family, we cannot make them fit into our fantasies of self-importance. Again, no matter what emotional survival game we play, it will render us the very results that we are trying not to get. Just ask yourself, are you getting the results you are trying to get in relationships?

CAPTURE YOUR THOUGHTS ABOUT MARITAL GAMES

Jealousy, Extra-Marital Affairs

The <u>cheating game</u> is so pervasive in our society today that it is common to place the blame on our mates. Many of us play a subtle <u>emotional bridging survival game</u> where we keep our hands in other pies in order to avoid loneliness or depth of loss as experienced by children. Somehow spreading ourselves around feels less threatening to the emotional psyche than giving our heart to one person. After all, giving ourselves to one person means that they will go away and if they go away somehow we will not be able to survive and will die.

In actuality most of us think a committed relationship is the end, with no idea of what is supposed to happen after the commitment. There is also the social status expectation and demonstration about committed relationships where we somehow think we are going to walk around with our mate who loves us for all to see. We have little guidance except for the previous map of how our primary caregivers interacted with each other and of course the television examples. So for the most part we do whatever feels good and when it no longer feels good, we quit and blame our partner, which correlates with our own issues.

Gumshoe Detective

Mac was quite an interesting character. He was the court jester at any given moment or time as well as charming and silly. He also was a thirty-seven year old bachelor who had never married which was not surprising given his relationship rules that ranged from warp, distorted, perverted, unconventional, preposterous, unbelievable and nonsensical. However, he meant no harm to the many women he had encountered over the years.

Mac never ended any of the broken relationships. His mates would slowly go away after the realization that Mac was Mac. His whole desire was to please and bring smiles to others' faces. He met and dated Serena for about six months before deciding that he wanted her close to him. He invited her to move in which she happily accepted and obliged shortly afterwards. One Saturday morning while the two were in the car driving from destination to destination taking care of errands, Mac's cell phone rang. He answered the phone and greeted the caller with great enthusiasm but somewhat of a whispering tone. *"Good morning, well how are you? Yes, you know I was going to get back with you…I meant to call you. I cannot talk right now… I am going to call you later this afternoon."*

Well by the end of Mac's phone call, Serena was hot. She had been sitting very close to him and could hear bits and pieces from the female caller, who had identified herself as Sandy. She had also heard the caller say that she really needed to see him and asked if he could come by that afternoon.

Of course Mac being the court's jester told the caller that he knew it had been awhile and they were going to get together later that day. Although Serena was unable to hear all of what the caller had said, she surely had heard Mac's responses to include verbal tones. Serena interpreted his tone and verbiage into Sandy being a special person in her lover's life.

As Mac rushed Sandy off the phone, Serena sat quietly and tried to hold her thoughts. After about three minutes of trying not to pry, she asked Mac the identity of the caller. Of course he in all of his character told her that it was simply a friend. Oh, that put Serena in frenzy as she further pursued the nature of the friendship. Mac responded with *"Oh, just someone I met a couple of years ago."* Serena replied, *"Oh, she is just calling out of the blue?"* Mac continued to explain that Sandy and he talked from time to time; sometimes every other month. This was clearly not satisfactory to his girlfriend as she further questioned him regarding the purpose of the call and his lady friend's knowledge about her presence in his life. Mac told Serena that he did not go around telling everyone his business.

By now she was even hotter and had already been somewhat suspicious of Mac's strange behavior over the past two months they had lived together. Now as far as she was concerned, her suspicions were being confirmed by this strange phone call as she felt that Mac was being evasive and omitting something about his friendship with this caller.

Serena decided to leave the issue alone for the moment, but not for long. She was going to confirm her suspicion of Mac's strange and erratic behaviors by identifying the infamous caller. As they reached another destination Mac got out of the car, leaving his cell phone behind as he entered into a business establishment. Once he disappeared into the establishment, Serena slowly picked up the telephone, confirmed the time and wrote down the number of the last caller. She could hardly wait to get to a place where she could call that number.

After Mac and Serena completed their outing, he dropped Serena off at their home and told her he needed to take care of an additional errand. She became even more furious. Scanning through their home caller ID, she saw that the number had appeared several times over the past week and earlier that morning. By now Serena's fury had increased to calling the number. She was nervous and did not know what she was going to do once the person answered. As the voice answered with a business greeting of a local loan company, Serena asked for Sandy. The person told her that Sandy had stepped out and would return shortly.

Serena was now certain that Mac had gone out to meet her. She decided to go to the loan company and meet the infamous Sandy upon her return. Serena in all of the uncertainty that someone could really love her drove hastily to the company with a mission to find out if Mac was seeing this woman on the side.

As she arrived at the loan company on her <u>never or not quite good enough mission</u>, she introduced herself as Mac's wife and asked for Sandy. The receptionist informed Sandy that Mac's wife was there to talk with her about him. Sandy was happy to see Serena and greeted her by asking if she was there to catch up Mac's account. She informed Serena that if the past due amount was not paid in the next few days, she would have to take possession of his collateral property made to secure the loan. Serena asked how much was past due, wrote a check and quickly left the loan company.

Of course we know that she must have felt silly at her assumptive attitude after finding out that Sandy was no more than a frustrated loan officer. Sometimes we tend to react illogically to our own assumptions that we are not good enough or are missing something that is preventing others from loving us. When we react in this irrational manner, we limit our ability to generate solutions to what we think is a problem. What Serena did not recognize was that if Mac was cheating, that was the least of her problems. The greatest of her problems would have been her self emergence into an already chaotic situation if her suspicions had been confirmed. The catch is what she would have done if there was evidence that Mac was breaking the rules of their co-existence. She had choices, but her problem solving turned into Serena the gum shoe detective.

What happens when the dynamics and elements do confirm our suspicions? What would Serena have done next? Was she really trying to confirm cheating on Mac's part or that she had what it would take to hold on to him? What story was she telling herself after going through the rigmarole of being angry, yelling, screaming and storming out? Some would say that is what Serena gets for not trusting Mac and for checking up on him. The outcome does not matter. What matters is what her efforts were all about. It was about her emotional ability or inability to <u>survive</u> this challenge of indiscretion.

Again, no one gets through life unscathed. If she truly believed Mac had broken the rules in their relationship then she had a choice to stay or go. Her responsibility was not to entangle herself in the alleged chaos. Serena needed to ask herself some real tough questions and be open for the truth in order to get the proper relief that was needed to survive this event. Now does this mean that she would not have felt sad, angry, mad or other emotions upon learning of an affair on Mac's part? No. But she could have considered what emotions she was reacting to and what thoughts precipitated those feelings. Did her insecure fears that she was not good enough generate the uncomfortable feelings?

An honest inner dialogue was the only way for Serena to establish the truth behind what was going on inside of her head. Once she would have done that, her emotions would have automatically changed and fit to the truth, allowing her to respond logically and with a clear head.

Would she have felt angry and upset at Mac's dalliance if it had occurred? Yes. We are human and will experience uncomfortable emotions upon betrayal by our mates. Again, it is how we react to those emotions that will determine how we cognitively process and interpret the indiscretion. Serena was reacting to feelings associated with distorted conversations in her head which the alleged affair triggered regarding things that she did not like about herself.

In her mind, since those things were broken it would have been the cause of Mac's cheating. Wrong!

Avenger

Sometimes the way we respond to confirmed indiscretion in a relationship may appear chaotic and really crazy as we try to make sense of what has happened. Daniel was extremely hurt when he had learned of Sheryl's unfaithfulness. One afternoon Sheryl called and reported that she had to work late. Daniel being suspicious of her ongoing late nights at work decided he would discreetly wait outside of her job to see if she would leave early or meet someone. He confirmed his suspicion as he watched Sheryl get into a vehicle with a man and kissed him.

As they drove off, Daniel followed and chased the vehicle in order to confront them. As he cornered the pair, he immediately attacked her lover, keyed his car and drove off. After returning home, he threw Sheryl's personal belongings out on the front lawn and called her to request that she quickly get them off of his property.

Prior to Daniel confirming her betrayal, Sheryl would tell their relatives and friends that he was paranoid, crazy and did not trust her. She would also tell them that he would not allow her to go places and questioned her on various whereabouts. She even suggested that he was bipolar and needed help. Oh that ole bipolar accusation by non-professionals is one of my pet peeves.

Daniel being unaware of her manipulative attitude often fell into her scheme and would appear as if he was crazy; when he did not find any evidence he often questioned his own sanity. When he would find unusual things, she usually gave such a good explanation that he just accepted it. However as time went on, Daniel slowly realized her inconsistency and that his suspicions were probably correct.

Later that evening of the confrontation, Sheryl returned home with her lover to collect her things. Daniel still on a rampage called her unpleasant names and told the lover that she was going to do the same thing with him some day. As they exchanged verbal blows, Daniel verbalized that he knew he never should have gotten involved with her.

We can clearly see that Daniel was upset. But what was going on with Sheryl that she simply did not end the relationship with him prior to starting a new one with her lover? What did she need from Daniel that prevented her from moving on? Why did she have a need to portray him in such a negative light? For Daniel, Sheryl exacerbated the issue by trying to turn the tables on him instead of taking responsibility for her actions. Torturing him was her need to avoid uncomfortable emotions as she crossed over into her next relationship.

Bridging

Yes, she was playing the bridging game to avoid a void between relationships. As Sheryl explained her perspective, she did not want to hurt Daniel's feelings; after all he had been good to her five year old son whose birth father did not pay child support. Was she really concerned about hurting his feelings? Or was she trying to circumvent getting blamed for ending the relationship by putting Daniel in a situation where he would get the hint and end it himself? If he ended it, then she would not have to feel bad; therefore, she was not the bad person.

Daniel's vulnerability was his effort to fix his past as he had been abandoned by his mother and his father exposed him to the ills of several potential stepmothers prior to sending him to stay with his paternal grandparents. In his relationship with Sheryl, he attempted to rescue himself by trying to rescue her young son from being moved from home to home. Daniel did not want him to suffer the same emotional distress that he had suffered as a young boy.

Now without knowing Sheryl's background, we can say for sure that she was trying to survive some form of emotional torment as she created havoc at each move and blamed the men. So as Sheryl again moved her young son into the home of another man, we know that she will continue to represent herself as a victim and transfer unaware and unfinished family of origin issues into the new relationship with her lover. Be aware that the <u>bridging game</u> is a nasty and self-centered game without any consideration to the partner; so if you see Sheryl's characteristics in your own relationship, save yourself time and trouble by making logical decisions over reactive decisions.

For the most part, what keeps us in relationships where we do not feel safe is we think we do not have any other choice or believe we are not good enough to meet someone better and have a healthy relationship. If we decide to stay, we need to understand the type of situation we are agreeable to as we expose our vulnerable feelings. Not only that, but is our staying a compromise of our values in an effort to think that we are good enough or after all do have what it takes? If we decide to stay, our role is not to become police officers, detectives, parents, undercover agents, or to fix and change our mate. The decision is to either listen to the distorted conversations in our head; or unravel the lies and tell ourselves the truth as we correct errors on our part and make appropriate changes wherever we feel necessary.

Play It Safe

Some of us tend to play the <u>safe game</u> after a painful loss as we try to avoid connecting with others by pursuing married individuals, or others whom we know cannot make a long term commitment. Carmen thought she could play this game after several painful breakups. However it backfired on her when Milton took the <u>confused stance</u> after being confronted by his wife Vivian, regarding his relationship with her. Vivian had found out about the two of them and gave Milton an ultimatum. He told Carmen that he still had feelings for his wife and did not know who he was going to choose.

Carmen's emotional vulnerability was so strong that she continued to justify her being with Milton by blaming Vivian for his affair. She used earlier criticisms from Milton when they first started seeing each other regarding Vivian's alleged inabilities or lacks of in the marriage to promote her own self-worth. Carmen believed that Milton would not have sacrificed himself if she was not better than Vivian.

As she watched Milton go back and forth between her and his wife, her self-worth increased as she promoted her significance in his life. What was interesting about her <u>self-worth inflation game</u> to feel significant was that she took risks as she sacrificed her mind and body to prove that she was more important than his spouse. As Carmen continued her futureless relationship with Milton, she failed to realize that he had violated his own commitment to love his wife for better or worse as well as did not resolve one relationship before starting a new one.

Emotionally Hostage

Another strategy of the bridging game is where we hold our partner <u>emotionally hostage</u> as we subtly seek out our own self-importance by soliciting various emotional responses from them. We tend to play this game when we are aware of their personal issues and use it against them as we accuse them of being jealous, crazy, and paranoid. As we watch them struggle to make out what the truth is, our emotional distress is relieved that we are wanted and have such importance with our mates.

The more our mates protest and confront us in their efforts to get clarification of our estranged behaviors, the more our insecurities are satisfied and relieved that we are so wanted. Our lying and hiding things from our loved ones is an outcry for self-importance.

**CAPTURE YOUR THOUGHTS ABOUT
JEALOUSY & EXTRA MARITAL AFFAIRS**

Divorce Games

Our society has experienced over the last twenty to thirty years a steady increase of divorces where nuclear families are rarely heard of and blended families are the norm. We have also subscribed to noncommittal attitudes which do not stride for committed relationships but rather loosely connected ones. We blame our partners for either working too much, being emotionally unavailable, being too fat or unattractive, not making enough money for the social class we want or for just not being able to meet our needs.

Many folks have an opinion on what works for men and women in relationships but none seem to hit the mark that has improved our ability to find a compatible mate for a long-term commitment. Although plenty of relationship advice and information gets released into the world, it somehow manages to get swooped up by the relationship vultures before its delivery. If you do not believe this, do your own assessment on the relationship sustainability of five to six people from every group environment you attend (to include personal, work, church, clubs, committees, and or boards). You will find at least three to four are divorced and the other two to three are struggling to stay together.

Religion used to play a significant part in families staying together, but in today's time partners change as the seasons change, religious or not. Yes, that is right. Look again at those five to six folks in your social, spiritual and work circle, married or not, and you will see that within the last twelve months, at least two have changed partners at least four times. The other three may not tell you about their secret rendezvous. Interestingly, it used to be about getting to the greener grass, but nowadays the changes are easily provoked by a person's mood change. If they do not feel happy, it is time to get a divorce or new partner. Loyalty to committed relationships is long in the past and we wonder why couples get prenuptial agreements.

Many are driven by such a high level of anxiety and emotional tragedies when it comes to relating that they ultimately sabotage their ability to align, bond and commit to others in all sorts of relationships; not just the intimate ones. The anxiety keeps them pacing indecisively back and forth regarding their self-worth on so many levels that ultimately it renders them failure in settling down. I attribute some of this anxiety to undiagnosed mental health issues but for the most part, society's many faulty expectations.

Loss of a relationship is worth crying over; it is a normal response and matches the event. To grieve is quite normal. However, in our society we somehow are not in control if we are experiencing uncomfortable feelings from that loss. We would think that once the marriage is over the games stop. Yet for some of us, the games intensify as we set out to prove we were good enough or to confirm that we were not. Other times we accept our demise of the marriage and play games to counter our fears of bonding to others.

Rites of Passage

One pervasive emotional survival game we play after divorce is the <u>best friend game/rites of passage;</u> it is interesting how serious some of us take this game. The basic concept of this ESG is that after divorce we can now get along with our ex-mate versus inside of the marriage; which is just our way of coping with the loss of the relationship as we try to move forward. It would seem logical to the concept of marriage that the friendship would have been a plus and strength within.

On the surface this game may appear very cool and cordial. But in actuality, sometimes the underlying motive is not about friendship. Part of the footing in playing this is that it gives us a sense of power and importance in our ex-partner's new relationship as their new partner struggles with the sincerity of the new found friendship.

Another prevalent game played after divorce is the safety game, which is similar to the staying and great friendship game. An outsider may see the behaviors as arrogant, but in actuality it is an intentional and deliberate tactic of emotional defense to avoid rejection and feeling like a failure.

In the safety game the partner finds that they can stop short of a long-term commitment and life will be good as long as the partner goes along with the plan. Generally persons involved in this strategy are viewed as good looking, self assured, upwardly mobile and able to bring something to the table. If one does not look closely enough, it may appear to be narcissistic as evidenced by the non-committing stance, evasiveness, selfishness, deviant behaviors and stuck-on-stupid responses that are displayed.

This partner usually is very pleased to spend time and enjoy your company at their convenience and they expect you to be satisfied. They think you should be available to them because no other partner before or after them, if they decide to let you go, can ever satisfy you or bring joy to your life again.

This person is your yen, alpha, and omega. Wow, they sound like a god, and aren't you glad that this partner blesses you with their presence when they feel like it? They need someone low maintenance due to their own high maintenance self. After all, how can they take care of you and themselves as well? They love someone who is confident because that makes the game all the more fun to play.

They will tell you to come watch the stars with them but you will need to drive, because what star drives to their own performance? This partner does not want anyone without a formal education and who cannot take care of themselves; but at the same token, if their partner exceeds them financially or in social status, then it becomes competitive and you will find them cheating with someone with far less income or status. Not that these folks are lesser citizens, but once this partner has been surpassed in their own high standards, they will want someone who is considered lowly to look up to them the way that you used to.

When this happens, run for daylight or prepare yourself for the crap they will heave onto you to eliminate any emotional threat in this game. Take for example Samantha who works at a local department store as a lead Cashier. She met this very charming, twice divorced, upwardly mobile Lieutenant in the military. Since the relationship began, he had been promoted three times. Now a Major, he is in command, not only of a unit of hundreds of soldiers but of Samantha as well.

She spends many hours trying to reassure herself and everyone of the security she feels with the Major. She has a key to his house, pictures of the two of them together on the walls and a drawer with a few overnight accessories. Now according to him, they are not at odds with each other and the minimal time spent together is due to the nature of his job where he is away from home quite a few days. Samantha continues with the day to day upkeep of his home and occasionally hears "I love you."

Although she suspects the majority of sextra curricular activity outside of the relationship, she increases her presence and photos at his house more and more; she knows that one day if she continues to give him the best part of herself, he will eventually marry her and make her complete. One Christmas, he even gave her a diamond ring. Nevertheless, no plans or date was set or better yet, no question was asked.

One day the Major was congratulated on his intent to marry and was asked why he kept such a secret. He professed that it was a simple gift, because she requested a ring. Unfortunately Samantha thinks it means more and is waiting for the day that he comes home on one knee and begs the question of marriage. Six years later, still no proposal. The Major is going about his life in search of joy. He was not at odds with Samantha but was content with his life and not trying to change anything; he just wanted to add a little joy through sports and outside affairs. He had already proven that he was at the pinnacle of his career.

All of his awards and accolades only validated that he was a man of integrity, great strength and intelligence. The only thing missing was a mate that epitomized all that he stood for. Apparently Samantha did not cut the mustard despite being pretty, kind and willing enough. She did not satiate his appetite. She was willing to wait for him to find what he wanted, yet how could he discover that if he did not know what he was looking for? The Major was able to identify in his search for joy that passion was missing from his life.

Better than Nobody

Samantha continues to hang in there while her lover still refuses to make plans toward a committed relationship. So what game is *she* playing? Is it the <u>Better than nobody</u> relationship game? It seems to be the script of modern times because it is so widespread in our society today in our efforts to rid of loneliness. Is she <u>watering the garden hoping that it will grow</u>, with a thought pattern that the natural order of things is that if you nurture it, it will grow? We are attracted to what nurtures us in our emotional life. It is like friends in the sand box that nurture each other through play but can not take care of each other. That is partly why the great friendship game is so easy for us to engage in because it is play, and playing is a distraction from distress. The problem arises here where some folks get stuck in the sandbox.

As we attempt to obtain the needed emotional growth, we tend to gravitate towards the nurturing that we missed from our family of origin. We learn who we are as well as our emotional age in our interactions with each other. We learn our strengths, challenges, vulnerabilities and so much more through those relations.

Hide and Seek

Tiffany, a thirty-eight year old divorced professional, played the hide and seek game; this is another ESG where one partner hides their objectives and feelings while hoping that they will get a specific payoff from the transaction.

In this game Tiffany was looking for Mr. Right for marriage. She had her share of dating various races of men and grew tired of dating the player players, Mr. USA's, losers, sex gods and a wide range of foolish lovers. She had gone through the superficial exchanges and was ready to settle down in a relationship of substance and newness. She met Shane, a 45 year old who was fairly different, consistent, affable, very gentle and a good conversationalist. During the course of the relationship however, she noticed several characteristics such as him being overweight that turned her off. In her incognizant game of hide and seek, Tiffany really thought she could get involved with Shane in spite of his increasing weight gain and could help him to lose the weight;

After all, she was a nurse and was very attracted to his sense of attentiveness.

Early on in Shane's effort to secure the relationship, he began making long-term financial goals that included Tiffany even as soon as two to three months into the union. However, as time passed between them, the attentiveness started to irritate her. As Tiffany became more aware and honest regarding the personal needs that she was trying to fulfill through this coupling with Shane, the rose colored glasses came off and she began to gradually disengage from the relationship.

As she attempted to maintain a platonic friendship without sexual intimacy, her unsuspecting partner found it difficult to switch gears all of a sudden. Shane increased financial rewards hoping that somehow Tiffany would change her mind and return to the way things were. He also sent e-mails professing his undying love for her. The <u>hide and seek</u> game on Tiffany's part increased to the <u>sacrificial game</u> of *"How much are you willing to do for me?"*

What we know about Tiffany's family of origin is that her father was not a part of her life and one of her mother's boyfriends had been both verbally and physically aggressive in his interactions with her. Tiffany developed a poor sense of self worth as well as trust issues where she required men in her life to sacrifice themselves in order to prove their love to her. If they complied, she would gain a sense of emotional security that they would be able to maintain the commitment and neither leave nor hurt her.

Tiffany was also playing the staying game as well while betting on her nursing abilities to help Shane lose weight. In retrospect, as she reflected on this relationship, even if Shane had lost the weight she would not have stuck around anyway, because she entered into it for the wrong reasons from the beginning.

CAPTURE YOUR THOUGHTS ABOUT DIVORCE GAMES

Games Played in the Workplace

Our work environment is generally driven by knowledge, skills and abilities to meet job requirements; but is it possible that we play emotional survival games in our workplace despite our goal and effort to meet basic survival needs? Yes, it is very possible and actually more games are played at work than in our personal lives because of the hierarchy being the same set up as in a family. Although the hierarchy is supposed to present in the form of responsibility, in the work environment it is played out as importance, therefore, rapidly generating emotional vulnerabilities. The games may go unnoticed because of the alleged tone of professionalism that is promoted in order to maintain the job.

Often times when there are problems or conflicts in the workplace, we tend to attribute personality clashes as the source. The problem is our immature emotions playing into the personality development, ultimately misrepresenting the adult. By default, blaming personality clashes is an excuse because we do not know what else to say or the polite way of trying to explain conflicts on the clock. We are missing this conversation in our societal interactions.

Given that we spend at least a third of our time at work, it is safe to say that from time to time we are going to have differences with others. It is possible that those differences expose us to our inner distress as we are unaware of our emotional vulnerabilities and sensitivities; therefore we transfer personal and unresolved family of origin issues in the workplace the same as in other relationships.

The problem arises when our emotional vulnerabilities show up in our work relationships, which often times presents in the role of a child or a sibling when the interactions become a little sticky or complicated. Usually what may trigger these vulnerabilities are non-supportive supervisors or co-workers not carrying out their portion of responsibilities. The way I hear the immature emotions played out is when folks say their manager talks crazy to them, down at them like they're a child or yells at them. With these types of accusations it would appear that a manager is being rude and disrespectful to the employee. If the truth is told, when I take a closer look at both personal and professional folks who make such accusations, I consistently find entitled dramatic souls seeking a sense of importance in the work hierarchy as they do not feel heard or even important in the work group.

Now I agree as the next person that managers should not do the alleged aforementioned behaviors; they are not perfect and also have issues that leak over into the workplace. Generally when a manager acts, many folks tend to react with fear and intimidation thinking they are securing their survival needs. They generally end up resorting to _passive aggressive_ games toward the supervisor. They tend not to speak up and to withhold their thoughts until either they blow up, quit or seek out other employees to support their emotional needs, while declaring themselves as the victims. Why? Because relief is needed. The person they seek out is the staff on any level of the hierarchy that reminds them of a family member with whom they feel the most comfortable. This person is generally the one that is the easiest to manipulate to their victimized stance that others are treating them poorly.

The opposite of this example is when someone is emotionally mature and they simply recognize that their boss or co-worker is truly interfering with the ability to do their job. So they assertively take appropriate actions of problem solving and if met with resistance, use their rights through the proper chain of command with internal or external authorities. It is just that simple. Everything else is drama from immature emotions.

Conceal Inadequacies

Some folks feel so inadequate at work that they try to conceal their inadequacies by actually pursuing friendships or sexual relationships which ultimately give them a false sense of approval. Unfortunately, many supervisors (married or not) are very vulnerable to sexual solicitations that fill their own need of self-importance.

Although very sad, I have seen staff members take the inadequacy game as far as falsely accusing co-workers, just like they did with their siblings to compete for their parents' approval, attention and validation.

Then there are other workers who in spite of the knowledge, skills and abilities that helped them to get the job, still have a strong need for ongoing approval of their worth. They may seek it through ESGs such as workaholism to validate that they are good enough, or to avoid dealing with personal issues; this is often accompanied by a faulty belief that the issues will work themselves out.

Ego Muscle Flexing

The Ego Muscle Flexing game is where an individual has a strong need to have power through some form of idolization from others through their status at work. This need correlates with a sense of unimportance as their parents were too occupied with their own issues to properly nurture their (child's) sense of worth. It also requires ego stroking that is sometimes at the expense of others in order for the flexor to thrive.

The flexor often gets their need met through passive aggressive or aggressive attitudes in the work place. This game's ultimate goal is to get feedback that will carry enough impact to stroke the weak ego. Once stroked, the flexor gains some form of validation that promotes the idealized perspective of their existence.

When folks play this game, others may see them as very smart, bright, intelligent and cannot help but to love them. However, emotionally they are begging others to tell them how important they are. In their quest of self-importance, they may tend to come across as a know-it-all who has been everywhere and done everything, but all along is sitting on a mount of insecurities regarding their identity.

Take for an example Dr. Orkin, who received his Doctoral degree on the internet from a non-accredited school. He was very adamant about others addressing him as Doctor Orkin. On the surface it appeared that he was very knowledgeable about the job and everything behind the scene.

He often talked about how the system was broken and what the higher ups needed to do to address the problems. He would also declare that if the higher ups would listen to him then all would go well. The Doctor often bragged about his worth and how he could make more money elsewhere but the company really needed him for his degree. If he received news of tentative changes he would take credit and broadcast it throughout the company while ensuring each person that he had only told them.

Under his leadership, he monopolized all meetings with a narcissistic perspective of his significance as he displayed little interest in feedback from others. When others would bring about alternative feedback, he would find a way to turn it into his idea or give a story of why the solution would not apply and indicate political ramifications if the suggestion was implemented.

Many of this flexor's co-workers ingratiated him as they embraced the idea that he was a doctor while others considered him the workplace court jester. On one occasion in response to a complaint made against him, Dr. Orkin made a threat to give up his position if his boss accepted the complaint and followed through with a write-up. Of course this was his way of declaring his value above other co-workers. Not expecting his boss to follow through, he roared about the complaint throughout the office as he sought to confirm his eminence. The Doctor finally received his declaration of importance as his boss accepted both the complaint and his threat to leave the position. As he retreated to his now reduced position on the same level as his subordinates, behind the scenes he heckled and undermined the new leader in attempts to maintain his superiority.

Soliciting Supporters

Another subtle way of soliciting self-importance in a group or work setting is the I cannot stand on my own game, in other words building a bandwagon. This game is where an individual goes about soliciting supporters because they feel unheard or unwanted but all along has a motive to gain power and validate their existence or point of view. Although this game is very common in the office, it also stands out in church, work and various committee groups and falls under the category of manipulation as they plead their case of unfair treatment. You may think this game is played only on the part of employees, but I have witnessed this level of validation in upper management staff, leaving employees at their mercy.

For those who are vulnerable and have a strong need to belong or feel important, they tend to fall right into the manipulative and sneaky behaviors often displayed in this game. However, others recognize the manipulation and choose not to participate by staying clear of the solicitations.

Let's look at how this game was played out in an office setting with Adrian, a fifty-seven year old retired military Officer now working as an Administrative Coordinator for a marketing company with two Administrators, Cliff and Kathy.

Kathy is Cliff's supervisor. Adrian had already retired from his first career and was only working this job to supplement his military retirement income. He had gained a reputation in the workplace as being straight forward with a no nonsense attitude. For the most part, he remained logical as he encountered problems and interacted with others on the job. In his mind, to encounter a problem meant to generate solutions and move on.

One day Cliff approached him with a problem regarding the Administrative Assistants overly scheduling him with too many appointments per day. He also complained that he did not understand why they were not scheduling the same amount of appointments with his supervisor, Kathy. Adrian informed Cliff that he would take care of the matter and inform his staff of the problem. So he informed the staff and received feedback that Kathy's schedule only allowed a few appointments a day due to other administrative duties that limited her schedule. Adrian updated Cliff on his staff's feedback regarding Kathy's inability to take more. He assumed the problem had been resolved and moved on to other issues.

Yet a few weeks later prior to going into a meeting, Cliff walked into Adrian's office, closed the door and informed him that he had filed a complaint with the CEO regarding the differences between the two schedules. He also informed Adrian that he had included him and another Director from the agency to support his grievance. As Cliff continued to elaborate on his reasons for filing, Adrian was stunned that he had been included within it. Trying to maintain his professionalism, he informed Cliff that he should have talked with him about the complaint prior to including his name. He then informed Cliff that he had a meeting and would get back with him.

As Adrian tried to focus in the meeting, he became very angry that Cliff had involved him and felt as if he had been placed in an untenable position. As he reacted to this anger and tried to relieve this uncomfortable emotional experience, he called Kathy to inform her that he was made aware of a complaint against her with his name included without his knowledge. He informed her that he was not sure of all the content but wanted her to know that he had not been a part of the complaint. Kathy thanked him for the heads up.

However on the next day, she approached Adrian and accused him of taking a passive stance with Cliff and not holding him accountable for including him in the complaint. By now Adrian was baffled with regrets of even informing Kathy as he thought that he had not been understood in his effort to separate himself from the protest. The Coordinator shared his regrets in bothering her with the matter. They discussed it further and both gained more information about various behaviors on Cliff's part to include solicitation of other staff for his complaint.

As Adrian reflected on the issue, he realized that Cliff's original approach to him had been a solicitation for support as he had not been able to take a stand on his own to communicate the unhappiness to his boss. We can see that in this game Cliff was trying to relieve emotional distress related to his lack of confidence and importance, seeking supporters to validate his point of view and significance. Ultimately Cliff was searching for self-importance at the expense of others.

For those of us that are aware of the various games played in our work environments, we have a choice to either bandwagon or guide the players toward solutions that will ultimately teach them that there are healthier alternatives to manage their emotional suffering.

Maria's workplace was intense as she encountered Mario, whom she thought was purposefully trying to taunt and intimidate her at work. As long as she felt powerless to him, she was miserable and often intimidated by his behaviors. As Maria refocused attention on her own emotional experience in their interactions, she was able to identify the origin of the fear.

The physiological response that she often experienced in her encounters with Mario had re-exposed her to early childhood memories where she felt taunted and powerless to an uncle. When visiting with her favorite cousins overnight, Maria would feel frightened as her uncle would abruptly erupt into fierce angry rages with menacing behavior. Once she recognized the source of her fear, she took control of the corresponding emotions and began using humor as a way to counteract Mario's taunting conduct.

Wolf Games

Wolf games are pervasive and dramatic in the workplace as we draw an audience's attention away from us and it becomes focused elsewhere. These games are usually at the expense of others and take place in various forms.

- The Trash Talkers, Jokers - Keeping the spotlight off of us by loud talking or criticizing others. This is not to say that we have to wear a blunted mask or cannot have fun and tease others at work. Humor can help us survive stressful and uncomfortable events in the workplace, but when it is at the expense of others it is devious and our vulnerabilities show.

- Emotions on Sleeves - May react by saying *"Who are you talking to?"* or *"Do not talk to me that way!"* When we react in this manner, we don't feel good about who we are as we felt emotionally threatened at that time. When we are okay with ourselves, we do not have a need to one up or get back at others in front of an audience.

- <u>Emotional Outbursts</u> - Include sudden episodes of crying, screaming or yelling to keep others away from us as we take on a victim's stance.
- <u>The Gossipers, Complainers, Grumblers</u> - An obvious emotional survival game that again shines the light on others' issues while avoiding our own deficiencies and inadequacies. When we huddle and participate in the gossiping game, we are trying to <u>fit in and belong</u>.
- <u>The Fuel Burner</u> - We act as hecklers or critics as we create conflicts with our co-workers, trying to prove our importance as we keep our own issues from being highlighted.
- <u>The Lone Ranger</u> - *"Do not bother me and I will not bother you."* This is where we try to stay in the <u>shadows</u> by showing our presence as little as possible. The ones who play this game may feel uncomfortable with conflicts and learned to survive in their family drama by avoiding disputes and staying out of the way.

Sabotaging

There are some extreme emotional survival games in the workplace that may present in a vicious manner, where someone goes out of their way to destroy another's livelihood by *sabotaging* their work. This is done out of a need for power and control over the targeted person.

It would seem logical that whatever job position a person accepts they would simply work it and when no longer satisfied, they would move on. Because of their lack of confidence, they have a difficult time taking risks and pursuing other interests, so they tend to play it safe. However, they are the most miserable, unhappy, grumblers, hecklers and complainers all while stewing in their poor self-worth. Ultimately it creates barriers where they are phony and defensive in their interactions with others.

Entitlement

In the entitlement game, people feel that they are automatically next in line for a promotion due to their longevity on a job, gender or skin color. When the promotion goes to someone else they begin sabotaging not only the promoted staff but the entire work area. The entitled staff tends to bandwagon as many supporters as possible to support their stance. They generally play on the emotions of the wolf game players, as these players lack confidence and generally speak from a low self-worth stance when confronted by their supervisor for poor performance. This game is only as effective as the leader's awareness of it as they respond to the entitled staff according to their own emotional vulnerabilities, or better stability.

CAPTURE YOUR THOUGHTS ABOUT GAMES IN THE WORKPLACE

Callous Games

The most Despicable emotional survival games as a result of extreme injured emotions from traumatic experiences, may range from controlling, to violence or even holding others emotionally hostage:

- You are <u>Not</u> going to leave me
- If I cannot have you, no one else will
- You are mine
- You have a mind of your own
- Until death do us part

Individuals who resort to this level may present as cold, callous and aloof with no capacity to care or empathize with others. They are functioning extremely vulnerable, tightly coiled, on the defense and ready to react to any perceived threat as a result of their past traumatic experiences. In spite of the danger with this game, the individual is trying to relieve uncomfortable emotional distress the same as others. They still desire to have their existence validated. The more invalidated they feel, the more mistrust exists and ultimately they fail to align and bond with others. When additional violations occur, it re-exposes their extreme sensitive emotions to past traumatic events with minimal coping skills due to having no recovery intervention tools. Without the appropriate coping, their behaviors could range from aggression, deception, extreme manipulation, degradation, derogatory, predatory, stalking, leashing, and lashing out at others. They do things in a manner with no consideration or regard to their partners, co-workers, neighbors.

Aggression

Take Martin for example who learned of his girl Virginia's indiscretion in their relationship. He normally was very good at putting up a social front at the break up of a relationship. However, he finally reached a point where it was difficult maintaining that front. By now he had put his whole life into one human being, Virginia, with the expectation that they would be together forever.

When Martin learned that she cheated on him, he became so consumed in rage to the point that he was preoccupied with the break-up and had a difficult time letting go of her. It was even more of a challenge for him when he watched her moved on with a new partner, a former mutual acquaintance and confidant in their social arena. Not only did he feel betrayed by the two of them but humiliated as he suffered in silence watching them hanging out in front of him.

For Martin the out of sight, out of mind game would have given him some relief as he tried to recover from the affair. But his healing process was much harder because their very presence was a trigger to every other betrayal he had experienced from early childhood. Those experiences ranged from physical and sexual abuse from one of his mother's boyfriends, to mother being too drunk to pick him up on the weekend from his grandmother, the absence of his father, his prom date backing out on prom day and now a former confidant sleeping with his ex-partner. For him it was just too much and ultimately his breaking point.

Martin's consuming rage was festering by the story that he told himself as he felt that he was being annihilated by Virginia and her lover; it seemed they were flaunting their relationship in his face. As he would watch the two of them appear very happy with each other, he often reflected on all the things he thought was wrong with him that may have contributed to her indiscretion. His poor self-worth and consuming rage prevented him from seeing that Virginia's dishonest actions were not about him, even though she blamed him in her need to justify her deed. Blaming him was her way of trying not to feel any more uncomfortable as she went about relieving her own misery. It would seem logical that she would have simply ended the relationship prior to starting a new one. Yet she was in her own distress and played the <u>bridging game</u> to help her avoid uncomfortable emotions.

Martin, on the defense, ultimately physically attacked Virginia and her new partner with a bat catching them both off guard, killing her new lover. In doing so, he validated that <u>something was wrong with him</u> as well as <u>he was not good enough</u> and as a result annihilated himself with a restricted life of imprisonment. As the realization of his new lifestyle set in, he often resorted to suicidal attempts as he was unable to relieve the emotional distress within that was driven by his preoccupied theme of betrayal by everyone. Interestingly enough, Martin was unable to see that he had betrayed himself.

He escalated his emotional survival game by using Virginia's affair as external evidence that <u>he was not good enough</u> and therefore deserved some restricted, isolated, or unworthy punishment. It may appear that the indiscretion on Virginia's part was Martin's first attempt to validate his self-worth. But in fact he had tried on several occasions in his interactions with others to align, bond, or commit. As he exited each relationship, he either confirmed or left in confusion regarding his value.

Martin's story may seem horrible in its ending because he did kill himself, leaving a note that he could no longer live with the demons inside. He was not alone when it comes to past traumatic childhood experiences. There are other stories that are far more horrific as we have all heard of serial killers, rampant rampaging, abusers, rapists, murder for greed and others in their need for power, control and prominence. The way we respond to our undeveloped emotions will depend on the way we tell the story of our interactions, transactions, and encounters with others. We have a choice to respond as a Victim always on the defense from passive to aggressive responses, or a Survivor embracing each emotional impediment as we provide our emotions with liability in our relations with others.

CAPTURE YOUR THOUGHTS ABOUT CALLOUS GAMES

Managing Our Emotional Life

From all the characters' storylines above, we have learned that emotional disturbance can impair an individual's ability to appropriately interact with others.

Emotional liability is no more than a set of rules and wisdom that provides us with confidence and courage while preserving dignity, respect and integrity in our relationships with others. It helps us to put down our defense and respond as our true self. It reminds us that we are all human and will have challenges in this life. It also helps us to move toward our personal goals as we experience the appropriate emotional responses and tell ourselves the truth versus distorted, catastrophic and exaggerated meanings we tend to give to an event.

We all have been challenged with issues from our family of origin experiences and surviving them is not always an easy task; however, as each decade goes by we learn more and more that we are designed to manage emotional dilemmas from the past. Yes, even devastating pasts. Therefore when we admonish each other to put things behind us, it highly suggests that we know we have the ability to do so. The ultimate goal is not to dismiss our memories and history as if it did not happen, but to authorize ourselves to acknowledge, address and accept it for what it was in order to stay truthful to our unique design and purpose on earth. It is the very key to aligning, bonding and committing to others that are compatible to us for our life's journey.

Without those three authorizations, we are forever in a mental state of flux and confusion with no inner harmony. The family of origin in which we were born is not a mistake, but the very date, time, place and family is part of a spiritual plan for our life and emotional development is critical to its success.

When we are taunted by emotional dilemmas, we are distracted from key elements in our unique design and are ultimately blocked from our spiritual ability to align and bond to a compatible mate that was uniquely designed to help us carry out our life's purpose. We will either respond to others:

- Assertively with confidence, courage and ultimately maximize our true purpose.
- Passively, withholding our thoughts, ideas and contribution to the world, ultimately living in fear and in the shadows of others and in a victimized stance.
- Aggressively with lack of confidence to problem solve, a high need to control, blame and ultimately unable to bond with others.
- Passive Aggressively acting as if we are cooperating with others but with no follow through and ultimately stay stagnated and dragging around the ill feelings of a victim stance.
- Dishonestly as Lidia who when she left the nest responded to society in a dishonest manner, lying as a result of a childhood experience where she tried to avoid a whipping by lying to her mother about attending an event she was not allowed.
- Pending Doom, the same as Vera who lived her early adulthood in fear in any type of group setting as a result of her parents' volatile relationships.
- Substance abuse, the same as Lorna who lived most of her adult life as an alcoholic trying to cope with the suicide of her brother. She was given her first drink by her mother due to ongoing nightmares from his loss. Over the years, prior to therapy and addressing this loss, she had lost several jobs, homes and relationships due to her drinking.

Our family of origin is a rehearsal for the adult world. Our caregivers' attention or lack of attention to our emotional development can leave us with a lifetime of healthy or unhealthy emotional responses. If unhealthy, we will need to do internal work to improve our interaction with others and there is no getting around it. When Lorna stopped drinking and did her internal work, her judgment improved and ultimately she was able to counteract her separation and attachment issues in relationships. She rejected what no longer worked for her and started living her best life.

Remember, not everyone survives the family of origin experience due to either being murdered, severely abused or neglected and left with unstable mental illness that impairs their ability to align, bond and connect to anyone and most significantly carry out their purpose in life.

Throughout this book, the pronouns "we, us, our" were used in order for each one of us to take a closer look at our own emotional stance when we connect with others. The goal of *ABCs of Relationships: Emotional Survival Games* is not to blame parents, but to reinforce that our primary caregivers are responsible for nurturing and guiding emotional development that will later result in our ability to live in harmony with ourselves and others.

As we go about asking what is wrong with us and why we have such a difficult time with others, the answer lies in our emotional development. So, **free your emotional self to be your best self**, which will ultimately allow uncomfortable emotions to pass through your psyche realm, thus producing a wider range of emotional experiences and healthy intimate and interpersonal relationships. Peace and success in your journey as you address your own emotional distress and survival games via the *ABCs Rules and Wisdom of Relationships* and the *ABCs of Relationships* workbook.

ABCs RULES AND WISDOM OF RELATIONSHIPS

1. All <u>Humans will error, however, it is our willingness to correct those errors</u> and improve our ability to align, bond, and connect to each other.

2. Humans are <u>not always reliable or trustworthy</u>; therefore, we provide ourselves with <u>emotional liability</u> that protects us as we encounter human tendencies to make mistakes as we try to align, bond or commit to others.

3. <u>Human beings do exactly what they want to do</u> – we do not have to confuse ourselves about others' estranged, odd and weird behavior when we are trying to align, bond or commit to others.

4. Always <u>avoiding conflicts or confrontations</u> will interfere with our true ability to align, bond and commit to others.

5. Being able to <u>generate solutions when problems arise</u> is part of emotional maturity.

6. Just as we have a choice, <u>others have a choice to accept or decline</u> our desires. Notice we use the word "decline" versus "reject".

7. <u>Each one of us holds the power</u> in our lives to make whatever necessary changes are needed in order to protect our emotions as we interact with others.

8. As we <u>learn more about ourselves</u>, we are able to understand how not to put ourselves in situations that go against our own values and standards. We also increase our chances of meeting our personal goals i.e., careers, children or relationships.

9. It is to ok to say, *"I am scared... I do not want you to go away... I would love to have you in my life..."* but it is not ok to beg them to stay.

10. <u>It is the stories that we tell ourselves</u> about broken relationships, not getting hired, or any situation where we have been declined - When others do not include us in their life it does not make them bad people.

11. The goal is that we are able to interact with others and walk away <u>okay with ourselves and remain okay</u> when we are not with others. Maximizing this goal will counteract that desperate need to fit in with everyone.

12. Now that <u>we have survived</u> our family of origin experience, we are in charge of our life and no longer have a need for Emotional Survival Games (ESGs). Remember the games will render us the very results we are trying Not to get.

ABCs of RELATIONSHIPS WORKBOOK
IDENTIFYING & INTERRUPTING YOUR
EMOTIONAL SURVIVAL GAMES

Cynthia D. Moore
Master of Science in
Counseling Psychology
Licensed Professional Counselor

In order to determine what games we play or have played to survive emotionally in our adult interactions with others, we will need to take a self-inventory on our family of origin experience. The answers to the questions will help us understand how we feel about ourselves as a whole as well as our comfort zone with others. The self-assessment will take time but it will show you how to pay close attention to errors on your part that continue to repeat themselves in relationships.

RECAPTURE

Before we get started, let's recapture the highlights of what we have learned from the *ABCs of Relationships: Emotional Survival Games* regarding our interactions with others.

- We realized that something is wrong as we have <u>repeatedly</u> tried to align, bond and commit ourselves to others.

- By the time we have reached early adulthood, an internal dialogue has already developed into some form of <u>self-belief</u> about our self-worth, sense of belonging and abilities.

- Many folks have suffered <u>emotional turmoil within their family of origin</u> that remains unresolved and is often transferred into adult relationships.

- The emotional distress suffered is often the result of <u>unrecognized and unresolved issues</u> that are strongly associated with underdeveloped emotions that were not properly nurtured or guided during early childhood and adolescent development.

- We now realized that we have subjected ourselves to undesired situations as a way of <u>trying to cope with our own inner distress.</u>

- The emotional distress often <u>interferes with good judgment, our daily functions</u>, goals, jobs, careers, dreams and the ability to align, bond and commit to others in a healthy manner.

- We try to relieve our distress by playing <u>Emotional Survival Games</u> (ESG).

- These ESGs will <u>ultimately render us the very results that we are not seeking</u>; that is unhappiness with unmet goals i.e., career, marriage, children, intimacy, interpersonal relationships and overall purpose in life.

As you pledge to record your past, present and commitment to embrace your future with emotional liability, reflect on your thoughts, wants, needs, likes, dislikes, strengths, talents, challenges and other areas for change and growth.

Also, use the information gathered to understand what has contributed to the person that you are today. Remind yourself, you are in charge of your emotions and no matter what you unearth, you are okay. Some things you will unearth, you will feel proud of; other things, you may wish to forget, but it is a part of you.

Finally, use your past experiences not for blame but as a base from which to identify unintentional errors on your part in your efforts to survive emotional distress in your adult interactions with others. This ultimately will help you to maximize your true potential as you *free your emotions to be yourself and live your true existence*. Therefore, work the assignments with pride, for you are worth it.

We will start with you revisiting your family of origin experience. Daniel will help you walk through it as he provides examples of his revisited family of origin experience that helped him to finally understand why he had such a hard time letting go of Sheryl, after she repeatedly cheated on him. He will also share errors on his part that kept him repeating the same scenarios over and over from one relationship to the next.

Remember, this visit may evoke uncomfortable emotions. That is the point of the assignments. If you do not want to do this alone, ask for the assistance of a local Counselor, Spiritual Leader or someone that has proven integrity in your interactions with them. Remember that you are the in charge adult and can work each section at your own pace.

Step 1 – Your Family Distress

Let's start by identifying significant life events from your Family of Origin Experience.

Identify family of origin experience(s) / event(s) that occurred at different stages of your life from 0-18 years of age. Ex- foster care; adopted; physical abuse; sexual abuse – molested, raped, incest, death of parent, sibling or other loved one; parents' divorce, separation; domestic violence; family relocation or family gathering. Please do not forget about happy experiences as well. So let us start with Daniel's example:

DANIEL'S FAMILY OF ORIGIN EXPERIENCE		
AGE	EVENTS	# OF EVENTS
0-4	NO SIGNIFICANT LIFE EVENTS.	0
4-5	DANIEL'S MOTHER ABANDONED HIM.	1
5-8	FATHER SENT DANIEL TO LIVE WITH HIS PATERNAL GRANDPARENTS WHO FOUGHT A LOT AND SPENT VERY LITTLE TIME WITH HIM.	2
8-12	HAD A GREAT 12TH YEAR BIRTHDAY PARTY GIVEN BY MY FAVORITE UNCLE. SAME YEAR FAVORITE UNCLE PASSED.	1
12-15	TEASED BY PEERS AND COUSINS FOR BEING CHUBBY.	1
15-18	NO OTHER SIGNIFICANT LIFE EVENTS.	0
TOTAL		5

AGE	EVENTS	# OF EVENTS
YOUR FAMILY OF ORIGIN EXPERIENCE		
0-2		
2-5		
5-8		
12-15		
15-16		
16-18		
TOTAL		

Step 2 – Your Emotional Development

Congratulations, you made it through step one. Pat that back! Now that we have identified various life events from your family of origin experience, let's identify your thoughts, emotions and behaviors as a result of those life events during childhood.

As you continue to reflect on your family of origin experience, transfer at least 3-4 or all identified experience(s) or event(s) into this assignment and follow these five steps.

1. Identify thoughts you had or still have that are associated with those experiences. (Ex- It's my fault that daddy left; I am the problem; nobody loves me).

2. Identify the emotional experience you had or are still having as a result of the experience(s). (Example: angry, sad, disappointed, frustrated, anxious, mad, excited, relieved, happy).

3. Identify how you reacted to your emotions at that time (ex- temper tantrum, pouted, ran away, withdrew, physically/verbally aggressive, argumentative, bully, peacemaker, did not eat, over ate, cried, oppositional, alcohol/drugs, sexually active, poor grades).

4. Identify the emotional support you received.

5. In retrospect what did you need from the adults in your life?

Now if you are ready, let's continue this family of origin journey. Remember you are not alone. Daniel's example will help you to walk through your own emotional development by sharing his own process:

DANIEL'S LIFE EVENTS AND EMOTIONAL DEVELOPMENT	
LIFE EVENT	Age 4-5 Mother abandoned me. Age 9-10 Grandparents fought about my needs. Age 12 - Uncle Passed but had a great birthday before his passing.
THOUGHT(S) EXPERIENCED	I thought my parents did not love me, if so they would have stayed and not sent me away. I thought I did something wrong when my uncle suddenly passed.
EMOTION(S) EXPERIENCED	Sad, Angry, lonely, missed my uncle a lot, Confused and Scared, especially after my uncle passed.
ACTION(S) DISPLAYED	I remember getting in trouble for instigating fights in school, I also ate a lot.
EMOTIONAL SUPPORT RECEIVED AND FROM WHAT ADULT	My uncle when he was alive but after his passing, no one, because my grandparents were too drunk; my surprise birthday party was a day that I felt very special and important because everyone came together and made it about me.
IN RETROSPECT WHAT DID YOU NEED EMOTIONALLY FROM THE ADULTS IN YOUR LIFE	With my mother's abandonment, my dad sending me to his parents and uncle passing, I needed to know that it was not my fault and that I was not a bother to others.

Now it is your turn to target your emotional development:

YOUR LIFE EVENTS AND EMOTIONAL DEVELOPMENT	
LIFE EVENT	
THOUGHT(S) EXPERIENCED	
EMOTION(S) EXPERIENCED	
ACTION(S) DISPLAYED	
EMOTIONAL SUPPORT RECEIVED AND FROM WHAT ADULT	
IN RETROSPECT WHAT DID YOU NEED EMOTIONALLY FROM THE ADULTS IN YOUR LIFE	

Step 3 - Your Emotional Framing

Welcome back, you made it to step three, so give yourself a double pat on that back and congratulations again. Now you are ready to detect the phrases and expressions that framed your Emotional Being.

I know that was quite challenging to go back and unearth your thoughts, emotions and actions to your family of origin experiences.

So, pause for a moment and take several deep breaths in order to relax before we begin the third assignment. This part of the family of origin revisitation is an extension of assignment two and may be a little difficult for you, but it will play a vital part in the next step. It will require you to recall and <u>re-expose your emotions to phrases and various expressions,</u> i.e., verbal, facial, body language that you heard and saw throughout your family of origin experience. These phrases and expressions have contributed, shaped and framed both your internal dialogue and emotional state of being regarding your sense of belonging, self worth and abilities.

See Daniel's example on the next page as he continues to disclose his experience.

DANIEL'S EMOTIONAL FRAMING	
PHRASES, EXPRESSIONS AND FROM WHOM	**WHAT** WERE YOUR THOUGHTS OR FEELINGS ABOUT THOSE PHRASES AND EXPRESSIONS
My grandmother would say that I am just like my mom!!	Well, I did not know her and everything I heard about my mom was bad, so I thought and felt bad things about myself because after all, I was her child.
My grandparents often would ask, "What will the neighbors say?"	I did not care what the neighbors thought and somehow resented them.
One of my cousins told me that he overheard my grandparents say I was a "mistake".	I really thought that something was wrong with me and it was my fault for being born.
My grandparents would say that my mom leaving me was a low down dirty shame.	I often felt ashamed of myself for existing and causing them so much shame and embarrassment.
My uncle would tell me that I was his favorite nephew.	Every time he would tell me this, it made me smile and I would tell him I loved him.

Now it is your turn to detect phrases and expressions that framed your Emotional Being:

YOUR EMOTIONAL FRAMING	
PHRASES, EXPRESSIONS AND FROM WHOM	WHAT WERE YOUR THOUGHTS OR FEELINGS ABOUT THOSE PHRASES AND EXPRESSIONS

Wow, you survived the revisitation to your family of origin experience. You may experience mixed thoughts and emotions right about now. So before you start the next assignment, take a moment to jot down your current thoughts and feelings about revisiting your family of origin experience.

THOUGHTS

CHECK YOUR EMOTIONAL PULSE - HOW ARE YOU DOING AND WHAT ARE YOU FEELING?

IF THE REVISITATION WAS TOO MUCH FOR YOU, I RECOMMEND YOU TALK IT OUT WITH A PROFESSIONAL COUNSELOR OR YOUR CONFIRMED SUPPORT SYSTEM.

Step 4 – Your Internal Dialogue

Targeting Reactive Thoughts

Congratulations again. I'm so happy for you, your courage and bravery to finally put your past in your control and begin living your life. Now, let's see how your family of origin experience may have contributed to <u>your interpretation of your self-worth, abilities and sense of belonging</u> by identifying any reactive thinking that you may have transferred into your <u>adult interactions</u>. Try to recall thoughts you had about yourself at the time when you felt most vulnerable in your <u>adult interactions</u>.

Here is Daniel's example:

DANIEL'S INTERNAL DIALOGUE / REACTIVE THINKING	
I cannot keep others in my life.	If Sheryl cheated on me, that means I am not good enough.
This always happens to me.	Why can I not find someone to love me?
What is wrong with me.	No one listens to me.
I am no good.	Nobody loves me.

YOUR INTERNAL DIALOGUE / REACTIVE THINKING

Step 5 - Your Adult Interactions

Reflect on various interactions and responses on your part within those interactions from **age 19 and above** with mates, friends, parents, church members, business associates or partners, store clerks, supervisors, co-workers, neighbors, police officers, popular or famous individuals and so on.

Step 6 – Your Feelings

Identify emotions experienced during the interactions (Ex - nervous, anxious) Ask yourself if you have ever felt this feeling before; if so, when and what situations/experiences.

Step 7- Your Games

Identify Emotional Survival Games (errors) on your part in those interactions. Examples: When you were trying to align, bond, connect or commit yourself to others; or when a situation/relationship did not go as you would have liked; if and when you were laid off from a job; family reunion; dispute with a store clerk.

How did you initially respond to the emotional threat or uncomfortable emotion(s)? Ex - Withheld true thoughts, lied, had an hidden agenda, premeditated to fix the potential mate once captured, protested, increased phone calls, inhibited, ruthless and riotous behaviors, rowdy, loud, unruly, cried relentlessly, struck out, one-upped, retaliated, and/or competed. For additional expressions, please *Choose from the list of Emotional Dispositions that is included at the end of this workbook – Please feel free to add your own.*

Step 8 – Your Emotional Vulnerabilities

Match the emotional vulnerabilities (Reactive Thoughts) experienced in those interactions that contributed to the games (errors). Ex - fear of being inadequate or not being good enough.

See Daniel's example:

DANIEL'S EMOTIONAL SURVIVAL GAMES & VULNERABILITIES	
INTERACTION WITH WHOM	Girlfriend who cheated.
EMOTIONS EXPERIENCED	Angry, disappointed, sad.
ESGs PLAYED	Played the "on good behavior" game hoping that Sheryl would eventually stop cheating.
EMOTIONAL VULNERABILITY	When folks leave, being abandoned & domestic violence history.

Ok, are you ready? You will have an opportunity to do this task on three different interactions. Take your time because this is a very important step in releasing unhealthy emotions.

YOUR EMOTIONAL SURVIVAL GAMES & VULNERABILITIES
INTERACTION WITH WHOM
WHAT EMOTIONS DID YOU FEEL
GAME PLAYED AND HOW DID YOU INITIALLY RESPOND TO THE EMOTIONAL THREAT OR UNCOMFORTABLE EMOTIONS
WHAT WAS YOUR EMOTIONAL VULNERABILITY

YOUR EMOTIONAL SURVIVAL GAMES & VULNERABILITIES
INTERACTION WITH WHOM
WHAT EMOTIONS DID YOU FEEL
GAME PLAYED AND HOW DID YOU INITIALLY RESPOND TO THE EMOTIONAL THREAT OR UNCOMFORTABLE EMOTIONS
WHAT WAS YOUR EMOTIONAL VULNERABILITY

YOUR EMOTIONAL SURVIVAL GAMES & VULNERABILITIES

INTERACTION WITH WHOM

WHAT EMOTIONS DID YOU FEEL

GAME PLAYED AND HOW DID YOU INITIALLY RESPOND TO THE EMOTIONAL THREAT OR UNCOMFORTABLE EMOTIONS

WHAT WAS YOUR EMOTIONAL VULNERABILITY

Step 9 - Feedback

Congratulations again, you are almost at the finish line. Take a moment to find out **what you have learned about yourself through identifying various verbal responses that you have heard from others** in your adult interactions. Please include both comfortable and uncomfortable feedback. After identifying the feedback, report how you responded i.e., thoughts, emotions or behaviors.

See Daniel's example.

DANIEL'S FEEDBACK FROM OTHERS	
I have often been told that I am so sensitive.	My Response each time I heard that... I would withdraw, retreat and avoided interacting with those individuals as much as possible.

YOUR FEEDBACK FROM OTHERS	
OTHERS' FEEDBACK	MY RESPONSE

What Have You Learned About Yourself?

As we approach the end of this journey, let's take a moment to reflect on what both you and Daniel have learned about yourselves in your interactions with others.

Daniel's example.

DANIEL'S SELF-REFLECTION ON WHAT HE LEARNED ABOUT HIMSELF
Did you discover any unresolved issues from your family of origin experience that were transferred into your interactions with others? If so give a brief description.
Issue of abandonment.
Did you discover any undeveloped emotions in your interactions with others? If so give a brief description.
My anger had been so prevalent in all of my interactions, which was mostly displayed in a passive aggressive manner.
What pattern of errors (emotional survival games) did you find on your part where you tried to avoid uncomfortable emotional experiences during those interactions?
The games I played were the on good behavior; passive aggressive; bought lots of gifts.
Did you find yourself in a win or lose mindset trying to stay afloat or in the game during your interactions with others?
Yes, I always thought that I was losing. I would compromise what I really thought and felt to accommodate Sheryl or others to keep them from being mad at me. Because if they were mad at me then they would leave me.

Did you find any reoccurring theme on your part in different interactions with others?

Ultimately, I found myself repeating the same scenarios over and over trying to keep people in my life.

What characteristic(s) was damaged or harmed during your family of origin experience? Ex - integrity, strength, courage, self-respect.

My self-confidence and courage was damaged as I really believed that no one could truly love or accept me, which I supported with my history of abandonment. I further supported this belief by my father being unavailable to help me through tough times due to his own family of origin issues.

During your interactions with others, what characteristics inside of you were trying to repair themselves? Ex. self-confidence, courage, strength.

My self-confidence and overall worth was trying to repair itself as I debated whether to stay or leave from the relationship with Sheryl.

What are your thoughts now about your sense of self-worth, belonging and abilities?

I now know that I am okay in the absence of Sheryl and her cheating was not a reflection of my self-worth, but an error in her character as she is trying to relieve her own emotional distress.

NOW IT IS YOUR TURN TO REVIEW WHAT YOU HAVE LEARNED ABOUT YOURSELF IN YOUR INTERACTIONS WITH OTHERS.

Did you discover any unresolved issues from your family of origin experience that were transferred into your interactions with others? If so give a brief description.

Did you discover any undeveloped emotions in your interactions with others? If so give a brief description.

Did you find any reoccurring theme on your part in different interactions with others?

What characteristics were damaged or harmed during your family of origin experience? Ex - integrity, strength, courage, self-respect.

During your interactions with others, what characteristics inside of you were trying to repair themselves? Ex. self-confidence, courage, strength.

What are your thoughts now about your sense of self-worth, belonging and abilities?

Step 10 - *Interrupting the Games*

Congratulations, you have completed unearthing emotional barriers acquired from your family of origin experience. So now that your self-awareness has increased regarding your thoughts and emotional life, you are ready to interrupt self-defeating thoughts and subsequent behaviors. You can also take control of your emotions and become more authentic in your interactions with others. From the 9th assignment, choose four of your most intense interactions experienced and <u>rewrite your part of the interaction by deleting the emotional survival game(s) played and incorporate three of the ABCs Rules and Wisdom</u> to replace them. As you do this, remember to provide emotional liability so that at the end of each interaction you will walk away with an empowerment statement that includes self-preservation, dignity, integrity and respect.

Let's start with an example by using Serena, the Gum Shoe Detective who went to confront Mac's alleged lover.

Here are the Instructions for the Assignment:

1. Write the interaction.

2. Choose three of the ABCs of RELATIONSHIPS RULES and WISDOM

3. Rewrite your part of the interaction with the new rules and wisdom.

4. Write an empowerment statement of how you feel now that you have applied the Rules and Wisdom to the situation.

INTERRUPTING THE GAMES

EXAMPLE
Serena in all of her fears that somehow she was not good enough or was missing something that was allegedly preventing Mac from loving her, played the Gum Shoe Detective game to validate her worth in his life.

APPLY ABCs RULES AND WISDOM
Rule # 2 - HUMANS are not always trustworthy by NATURE SO if Mac is cheating then I need to protect myself.
Rule # 6 – I have a choice to not participate in this relationship, if I really believe that Mac is being indiscreet.
Rule # 7 - I hold the power in my life to make whatever changes are necessary to protect myself at this is time.

REWRITE YOUR PART OF THE INTERACTION WITH THE NEW RULES AND WISDOM

I am going to talk with Mac about my concerns and based on his response, if I continue to feel unsure of his intention in my life at this time, I am going to use my choice to leave with or without evidence of indiscretion.

EMPOWERMENT STATEMENT
I realize that if Mac is cheating, that this is a matter of character on his part and not a matter of my self worth. I am not powerless to this situation if indeed he has been indiscreet in our relationship.

INTERRUPTING THE GAMES

YOUR OWN SCENARIO

CHOOSE THREE ABCs RULES and WISDOM

REWRITE YOUR PART OF THE INTERACTION WITH THE NEW RULES & WISDOM

EMPOWERMENT STATEMENT

INTERRUPTING THE GAMES

YOUR OWN SCENARIO

CHOOSE THREE ABCs RULES and WISDOM

REWRITE YOUR PART OF THE INTERACTION WITH THE NEW RULES & WISDOM

EMPOWERMENT STATEMENT

INTERRUPTING THE GAMES
YOUR OWN SCENARIO
CHOOSE THREE ABCs RULES and WISDOM
REWRITE YOUR PART OF THE INTERACTION WITH THE NEW RULES & WISDOM
EMPOWERMENT STATEMENT

INTERRUPTING THE GAMES
YOUR OWN SCENARIO
CHOOSE THREE ABCs RULES and WISDOM
REWRITE YOUR PART OF THE INTERACTION WITH THE NEW RULES & WISDOM
EMPOWERMENT STATEMENT

WOW!! Great Job! You survived the revisitation of your family of origin experience. Now let's do the survey from chapter two again, but this time you get to score it in order to assess your current level of emotional vulnerability in your interaction with others.

Post Survey

1. I have adjusted and compromised my values to align, bond and connect to others.

Strongly Agree   Agree   Sometimes   Disagree   Strongly Disagree

2. I have often misinterpreted others' responses into my own fantasized value of their intention with me.

Strongly Agree   Agree   Sometimes   Disagree   Strongly Disagree

3. I have often had sex to avoid being alone.

Strongly Agree   Agree   Sometimes   Disagree   Strongly Disagree

4. I need to have discussions with others on how to interact with a person.

Strongly Agree   Agree   Sometimes   Disagree   Strongly Disagree

5. I have repeatedly tried to align, bond, connect and commit myself to others without success.

Strongly Agree   Agree   Sometimes   Disagree   Strongly Disagree

6. I have often asked myself what is wrong with me.

Strongly Agree   Agree   Sometimes   Disagree   Strongly Disagree

7. I feel a need to survive or plan a strategy in upcoming interactions with others.

Strongly Agree   Agree   Sometimes   Disagree   Strongly Disagree

8. I participate in gossiping.

Strongly Agree   Agree   Sometimes   Disagree   Strongly Disagree

9. I often say that I am too busy to go out or participate in events.

Strongly Agree   Agree   Sometimes   Disagree   Strongly Disagree

10. I talk excessively on the telephone to avoid being alone.

Strongly Agree   **Agree**   **Sometimes**   **Disagree**   **Strongly Disagree**

11. I have never cheated on my mate not even once.

Strongly Agree   **Agree**   **Sometimes**   **Disagree**   **Strongly Disagree**

12. I am aware of my challenges and weaknesses in relationships.

Strongly Agree   **Agree**   **Sometimes**   **Disagree**   **Strongly Disagree**

13. I do not lie to others to avoid uncomfortable situations.

Strongly Agree   **Agree**   **Sometimes**   **Disagree**   **Strongly Disagree**

14. I am aware of my strengths in relationships.

Strongly Agree   **Agree**   **Sometimes**   **Disagree**   **Strongly Disagree**

15. I am aware of my emotional vulnerabilities in relationships.

Strongly Agree   **Agree**   **Sometimes**   **Disagree**   **Strongly Disagree**

16. I am aware of the impact of my family of origin experience in my interaction with others.

Strongly Agree   **Agree**   **Sometimes**   **Disagree**   **Strongly Disagree**

17. I feel secure with my emotions as I interact with others.

Strongly Agree   **Agree**   **Sometimes**   **Disagree**   **Strongly Disagree**

18. I have remained faithful to my values and standards as I have tried to align, bond and connect to others.

Strongly Agree   **Agree**   **Sometimes**   **Disagree**   **Strongly Disagree**

19. I do not need others to validate my decisions.

Strongly Agree   **Agree**   **Sometimes**   **Disagree**   **Strongly Disagree**

20. I have settled in relationships to avoid being alone.

Strongly Agree   **Agree**   **Sometimes**   **Disagree**   **Strongly Disagree**

Survey Outcome

Let's see how you faired out and if there are any variances in your pre and post survey results. Total your scores to assess your vulnerability in your interactions as you attempt to align, bond, connect or commit to others.

0-20	Emotionally Secure
21-39	Mildly Vulnerable
40-59	Moderately Vulnerable
60-79	Moderately to Severely Vulnerable
80-100	Severely Impaired Emotions

Now do not get bent out of shape or overly excited with whatever you score because as we go through the various terrains of life, depending on our emotional foundation and support system, our vulnerability may vary.

GO AHEAD AND REVIEW THE NEXT FEW PAGES FOR THE VULNERABILITY CHARACTERISTICS AND SEE HOW YOU FAIRED OUT.

VULNERABILITY CHARACTERISTICS

CHARACTERISTICS 0-20
Emotionally Secure

You are aware of the impact from your family of origin experience and are able to manage emotional responses without infringing or imposing your emotional responsibilities on others. You feel secure within your emotions and do not take on others' emotional responsibilities because you recognize when it is your issue versus their issue. You also have realistic expectations of yourself and others in your interactions. You are able to stick with your values and standards in spite of peer pressure. You are open and able to take into consideration the feedback of others, including misdirected criticism. You are willing to take necessary risks to maximize your true potential. You are able to use wisdom in your interactions with others. You clearly understand the benefits of emotional liability.

SELF PRESERVATION	DIGNITY
GOAL ORIENTED	AWARE OF ENVIRONMENT
TRUSTS SELF	ASSERTIVE
COURAGE	NOT EASILY SWAYED
OPEN TO RISKS	FREE SPIRITED
CONFIDENT	ASSESSES SITUATIONS
SELF-ASSURED	INTEGRITY

CHARACTERISTICS 21-39
Mildly Vulnerable

You are mildly vulnerable, in one type of relationship setting such as work or social or intimate, but not all. You are able to recognize some interactions that evoke emotional distress associated with your family of origin experience. Although you have some awareness of your emotional vulnerabilities, you may second guess others' motives and react to your own vulnerabilities during your interactions with them. You recognize that you need to provide emotional liability in order to protect your vulnerable emotions.

GOAL ORIENTED	SPONTANEOUS RISKS
MINIMAL SELF-DOUBT	NICE SOCIAL GAMES
OVERACHIEVER	FIX THE PAST GAMES
LONE RANGER ATTITUDE	SOME ASSERTIVENESS
MINIMAL APPREHENSION ABOUT COMMITTING	MAY COMPROMISE SOME VALUES

CHARACTERISTICS 40-59
Moderately Vulnerable

You are moderately vulnerable to the risk of playing passive emotional survival games by subjecting and compromising your values in your interactions with others, which is simply too much power to give to anyone. Somewhat dependent on others' point of views versus your own. Tendency to take the avoidance route versus holding your own stance. I recommend building a support system that includes personal development and spiritual values that will help you to clarify what is right for you.

RELIES ON OTHERS TO CONFIRM YOUR WORTH	PLAYS PEACE SAKE GAMES
STAYING GAMES	EASILY WITHDRAWS
NOT GOOD ENOUGH	TENDS TO GOSSIP
BRIDGING GAMES INSECURE	AVOIDANCE
GREAT FRIENDSHIP GAMES	RIGHT OF PASSAGE
VICTIM STANCE	FIX THE PAST
ON BEST BEHAVIOR	AVOIDANCE
ATTENTION SEEKING	HIDDEN AGENDAS
EXCESSIVE TALKING	ROMANTICIZES

CHARACTERISTICS 60-79
Moderately to Severely Vulnerable

You are very vulnerable to participating in defensive, derogatory, degrading and demeaning responses in your interaction with others due to feeling emotionally threatened by them (i.e., giver or receiver). You have very little insight, if any, into your unrecognized and unresolved emotional issues. Your values and standards are based on a strong need to have power within the interaction as you may have felt powerless to some of your family of origin experiences. You may have felt unsupported and isolated as you tried to survive those experiences, which were too much for a young child without the proper adult or authority support and intervention. You may have tried to survive those experiences by drinking or other forms of substance use.

SELF-INFLATION	LYING
STAND OFFS	COMPLAINER
NOT GOOD ENOUGH	TENDS TO GOSSIP
EGO FLEXING	CAT AND MOUSE
ARGUMENTATIVE	RIGHT OF PASSAGE
VICTIM STANCE	CHEATING
DOMINATES CONVERSATIONS	WITHDRAWS A LOT
CONTROLLING	HIDDEN AGENDAS
ANGER OUTBURSTS	TEMPER TANTRUMS
POOR LISTENER	ENTITLED
VERBALLY ABUSIVE	FIGHTS
INTRUSIVE	RUDE

CHARACTERISTICS 80-100
Severely Impaired Emotions

Your childhood experience may have been very challenging, most likely without the best setting for childhood development. You are extremely vulnerable in all relationship settings (professional, social and intimate). At this level you are functioning in an emotional impairment zone. The games played here indicate a need for power due to feeling powerless to others; they often times lead to detrimental responses toward others and ultimately self-destruction.

I AM NOT GOING TO LET YOU GO	HIGHLY IMPULSIVE
IF I CANNOT HAVE YOU NO ONE ELSE WILL	SELF-HARM
HARM TO OTHERS	AGGRESSIVE
ISOLATES OTHERS	QUICK TO SNAP
EDGEY ALL THE TIME	SOME POSSIBLE SELF ISOLATION

YOUR NEW EMOTIONAL LIFE

Now that <u>you have taken the initiative to face off and address your</u> family of origin issues, it is time for you to test drive your new emotional life. But in order to do so, you will need to provide yourself rules and wisdom for your future interactions. As in all life events, there is a graduation in order to move forward. In this final assignment you will jot down several of your own rules and wisdom that you will incorporate from this point forward in your interactions with your family, circle of friends, social groups, spiritual and intimate relationships.

Keep in mind the rules you create must allow you to align, bond or commit to people that are compatible for you and do not go against your values, goals or the results you are trying to get in life. In other words, the rules will provide you with emotional liability as you interact in various settings. The rules are also free of harm to yourself or others. It is okay to update the rules as your emotions continue to mature.

Peace and Success in your Journey

of Inner Harmony as you

Align, Bond and Connect to others

who are compatible for you.

The final CONGRATULATIONS is on YOU!

From the Desk of Ms. Cynthia

YOUR PERSONAL RULES AND WISDOM
CIRCLE OF FRIENDS
SOCIAL GROUPS
FAMILY
INTIMATE RELATIONSHIPS

INDEX OF EMOTIONAL SURVIVAL GAMES

A
ABRASIVE
ANGER OUTBURSTS

ARGUMENTATIVE
ASSERTIVE
ATTENTION SEEKING
APPREHENSIVE ABOUT COMMITTING
AVOIDANCE

B
BEGS OTHERS TO STAY

BELITTLES
BRASH
BRAVERY
BRIDGING GAME
BULLYING

C
CAT AND MOUSE
CATTY
CONTROL THE CLOSENESS
CHEATS
COMPROMISES VALUES & STANDARDS
COMPENSATES
COMPETES
CONFIDENCE
COURAGEOUS
CRIES TO MANIPULATE OTHERS

COMPLAINER
CONTROLLING

D
DIFFICULTY HEARING OTHERS' FEEDBACK
DOES NOT WANT TO BE ALONE

E
EGO FLEXING
EMOTIONAL OUTBURSTS
ENTITLED
EXCESSIVE TALKING

F
FEARFUL
FIGHTING
FUEL BURNER
FIX THE PAST

G
GIVING MONEY / GIFTS
GOSSIPING
GREAT FRIENDSHIP
GRUMBLER

H
HIDE AND SEEK
HIDDEN AGENDAS

ABCs OF RELATIONSHIPS

I

I AM THE BOSS OF YOU
IDOLIZES
IMPULSIVE
INCREASED PHONE CALLS
INSENSITIVE TO OTHERS
INSTIGATES
INTERRUPTS
I AM NOT GOING TO LET YOU GO
IF I CAN'T HAVE YOU NO ONE WILL
I AM GOING TO LEAVE YOU
BEFORE YOU LEAVE ME

J

JUDGMENTAL

K

KIND

M

MANIPULATIVE
MACHIAVELLIAN

L

LEGALISTIC
LITTLE SELF CONFIDENCE
LONE RANGER
LYING

N

NICE SOCIAL GAMES

NOT GOOD ENOUGH

O

OVER ACHIEVER
ON BEST BEHAVIOR
ONE-UP

P

PEACE SAKE
PLEASE COMMIT
POUTS
POOR LISTENING
PREMEDITATE TO FIX POTENTIAL
MATE

Q

R

RELIES ON OTHERS OPINION
RIGHT OF PASSAGE
RUTHLESS
ROWDY
RUDE

S

SACRIFICE
SECURE THE RELATIONSHIP
SELF-HARM
SELF-INFLATION
SELF- PRESERVATION
SHADOW GAME

SPONTANEOUS RISKS- such as
gambling pertinent income

STAND OFFS

STALKING

STAYING GAME

STRIKES OUT

U

V

VICTIM STANCE

VERBAL ABUSE

W

T

TEMPER TANTRUMS

WITHDRAWS

WIITHHOLDS TRUE THOUGHTS

WALKS AWAY FROM SITUATIONS